ROBERT BURNS'S TOURS OF THE HIGHLANDS AND STIRLINGSHIRE 1787

Robert Burns's Tours
of the Highlands
and Stirlingshire 1787

RAYMOND LAMONT BROWN

The Boydell Press · Ipswich · 1973

PUBLISHED BY THE BOYDELL PRESS LTD
PO BOX 24 IPSWICH IP1 1JJ SUFFOLK

ISBN 0 85115 019 5

PRINTED IN GREAT BRITAIN BY
THE ANCHOR PRESS LTD, AND
BOUND BY WM. BRENDON & SON LTD,
BOTH OF TIPTREE, ESSEX

Contents

Illustrations

Between pages 34 and 35

Endpaper Map: Robert Burns's Tours of the Highlands and Stirlingshire

Acknowledgements

A special word of appreciation is due to the following library authorities and institutions, and their librarians, for their kind help, advice and permissions: Argyll County Council, Education Committee; County Council of Dumbarton, Education Committee; County Council of Stirling; Burgh of Falkirk; Royal Burgh of Stirling, Public Libraries Dept; Perth and Kinross County Library; The Corporation of Glasgow, Libraries Dept; Inverness County Library; The Corporation of Dundee, Public Libraries Dept; Aberdeen County Council, Education Committee; County Library, Elgin; Arbroath Public Library; Angus and Kincardine County Councils, Joint County Library Committee; Inverness County Library and Museum; Banff County Council; National Library of Scotland; University of Edinburgh, School of Scottish Studies; Peterhead Public Library and Arbuthnot Museum; Aberdeen City Libraries; Edinburgh Corporation, Libraries and Museums Dept; Newcastle-upon-Tyne, City Libraries; and the University of Newcastle-upon-Tyne.

I am indebted, too, for advice, encouragement and generosity shown by the following at various stages of the manuscript's development: Miss C. H. Cruft, of the Royal Commission on the Ancient and Historic Monuments of Scotland, Edinburgh; The Town Clerk of Dumbarton; The Secretary to the Court of the Lord Lyon, Edinburgh; William Brown, Public Relations Manager of the Carron Co., Falkirk; Marie C. Jordan of the *Glasgow Herald*; R. Singer of the *Press and Journal*, Aberdeen; Lawrence R. Burness of the William Coull Anderson Library of Genealogy, Arbroath; the Glenbervie Burns Memorial Association; J. F. T. Thompson of the

Burns Federation; R. H. Watson of Aberdeen; T. McVittie of the Property Services Agency of the Dept of Environment for Scotland at Edinburgh; Alex E. O'Neill, Town Clerk of Bo'ness; Mrs M. P. Stevenson, Museum Assistant of the Scottish National Portrait Gallery; Dr M. H. B. Sanderson of the Scottish Record Office; The Earl of Elgin; and the Clerk to the Faculty of Advocates.

All the illustrations have been acknowledged separately, in the list of illustrations on pp. vii-ix.

DEDICATION

To my many friends in the Highlands,
and to the many people who have helped me
in my travels therein.
Conjointly I dedicate this book
to my friends the members
of the Berwick Local History Society
and the Berwickshire Naturalists' Club.

LIUBHAIRT

Do 'm luchd-eòlais air Ghàidhealtachd
is dhaibh-san a chuidich mi
ré mo chuairtean an sin. Maille riutha tha mi a' liubhairt
an leabhair seo do 'm luchd-eòlais,
muill Comunn Eachdraidh Ionadail Abaruig is Comunn
Luibheadairean Siorramachd Abaruig.

Introduction

'Your Lordship touches the darling chord of my heart when you advise me to fire my muse at Scottish story and Scottish scenes—I wish for nothing more than to make a leisurely Pilgrimage through my native country; to sit and muse on those once hard-contended fields, where Caledonia, rejoicing, saw her bloody lion borne through broken ranks to victory and fame; and catching the inspiration, to pour the deathless Names in Song.' Thus Robert Burns wrote in a letter to his would-be patron David Stewart Erskine, eleventh Earl of Buchan (1742–1829), from his lodgings at the Lawnmarket, Edinburgh, on 7 February 1787.

This heartfelt wish was attained soon after the letter was written. For on the receipt of several sums of money, consequent upon the publication of the Edinburgh Edition of his *Poems*, Burns was able to make immediate plans for travel. On 5 May 1787, in company with his lawyer friend Robert Ainslie (1766–1838), he started on a tour of the Borders.* A brief journey to the Western Highlands followed, then a more protracted six-hundred-mile tour of the Central Highlands and subsequently a tour of Stirlingshire.

The documentation of Burns's tours of the Highlands and Stirlingshire is made up in the following way. The tour of the Western or Argyllshire Highlands as far as Inveraray and his tour of Stirlingshire with Dr James Adair can be collated from the poet's own letters and from diary entries, notes and scraps of information collected by others.

---

* See: Brown, Raymond Lamont. *Robert Burns's Tour of the Borders*: Ipswich, Boydell Press, 1972.

Burns did not leave any journal entries for his tour of the Western Highlands, or his Stirlingshire jaunt, but as with his Border tour, Burns kept a journal for his tour of the Central Highlands. The original is a notebook measuring about 18 cms × 11½ cms, now containing 26 leaves. There are 35 pages of Burns's original script; seven, at the beginning of the volume, carrying the names of persons and places associated with the excursion; 28 contain the *Journal*; and the rest are blank.

As J. C. Ewing recorded in his unannotated facsimile of the manuscript (London: Gowans & Gray Ltd, 1927): 'From between the pages numbered 24 and 25 a leaf of the *Journal*, carrying the record of 10–13 September, is unfortunately now missing. That it was present in the volume when William Scott Douglas, editor of Burns, handled it is apparent from his printed text, though it was absent when the volume was sold at Edinburgh in 1887.' William Scott Douglas, of course, edited *The Works of Robert Burns* (Edinburgh, 1876–77).

Most of the script in the original manuscript is in ink, but parts were written by Burns in pencil; this portion was later inked over by the arch-meddler Dr James Currie (1756–1805), but the two lines at the top of the manuscript page 22 are an addition by William Scott Douglas.

It appears that the *Journal* of this Central Highlands tour was sent early in 1797 to Dr James Currie at Liverpool by the Burns Family Trustees at Dumfries. It was doubtlessly a part of that 'huge and shapeless mass' of manuscript material Currie (he refers to the papers in his letter of 8 February 1797 to researcher John Syme) had collected for his biography of the poet *The Works of Robert Burns, with an account of his life* (Liverpool, 1800). The *Journal*, however, was not heard of again until the entry in the 'Catalogue of manuscripts for sale', put up by Thomas Thorpe, the London dealer, in 1836: under the entry *Journal of the Scotish Bard's Northern Tour, Autograph MS., unpublished, £3 3s.*

The manuscript was subsequently in the extremely valuable collection of papers owned by James T. Gibson-Craig of

Edinburgh, from whom W. Scott Douglas had it on loan. On the dispersal of the Gibson-Craig collection (at Dowell's sales-rooms, Edinburgh, on 28–29 March 1887) the *Journal*, referred to as Burns's 'Diary kept during his Highland Tour', was purchased by William Brown, bookseller of Edinburgh, for £27 6s. It was thereafter owned by the London publisher John Murray, and then William K. Bixby (1857–1931), of St. Louis, Missouri, USA.

According to the *Guide to Archives in the United States* (New Haven and London: Yale University Press, 1961), compiled by Philip Harmer, William K. Bixby's collection is held at the Washington University Libraries, St Louis. But the holograph manuscript of Burns's Highland Tour was presented to, and is now to be found at, the Burns Cottage Museum, Alloway, Ayr. It is listed as Catalogue Number 166 under the title: *Burns Journal of his tour of the Highlands August–September 1787; the original journal, containing 35 pages in his hand-writing, which he carried in his pocket and wrote up as occasion permitted.*

The importance of the documentation and literary content of Burns's tours is of immense value to the student and researcher into Burns's life and works. For here we have Burns doing for once something that he really wanted to do, namely travel; and while in 'a high holiday mood', he allowed his mind to become undisciplined from toil, and just observe. This was an important development, for ordinary life for Burns was a continual round of frustration, with interludes for analgesics, like sex and poetrymaking.

What the tour journal and background holograph letters reveal of Burns the man in his own words, and the significance therein, is discussed in the Epilogue (pp. 59–63). In the meantime there follows, for the first time ever, a detailed account of his tours of the Highlands and Stirlingshire 1787, which in themselves make fascinating reading of eighteenth-century Scottish rural and urban life, recreation and travel: For as the late Professor G. M. Trevelyan pointed out, if anything at all, eighteenth-century man was 'a travelling species'.

Burns's Tour of the West Highlands

In mid-June 1787, shortly after he had returned to Mauchline
(8 June 1787) from his Border Tour, Burns set out alone for
the West Highlands, Mary Campbell's country.[1] As on his
Border Tour, he rode his mare 'Jenny Geddes'. His route for
this tour is uncertain and his real purpose unrecorded: Was it
merely spiritual boredom which made Burns suddenly embark
on this unaccountable journey? Could it have been made to
collect subscriptions still due to him, as his autobiographical
letter of 2 August 1787 to Dr John Moore from Mauchline
would suggest? Or had it something to do with a guilty
conscience through the death of Mary Campbell? At least
Dr F. B. Snyder hints at this in *The Life of Robert Burns*
(New York, 1932). Again, perhaps it began as a pilgrimage to
Greenock to seek out Mary Campbell's grave? Catherine
Carswell categorically says that this was the reason in her
romantic and largely unauthenticated *The Life of Robert
Burns* (London: Chatto & Windus, 1930). It must be remembered, however, that the tradition that Burns visited
Greenock during this trip and interviewed Mary Campbell's
mother is not corroborated with any documentary proof. In
all probability we shall never know Burns's motives, but some
vital clues to his movements can be built up from his letters.

Burns first visited Glasgow as a convenient starting place
for the west coast. Here he sent home some fine silk for his
mother and sisters, or so his sister Isabella (1771–1858) told
Robert Chambers. The first we can really learn of his travels,
however, is in the fragment of the letter of 25 June 1787 to
Robert Ainslie:

[5]

Arrochar, near Crocharibas, by
Loch Loang

My dear Friend & Brother Arch[*mason*]
    I am writing this on my tour through a country where
savage streams tumble over savage mountains, thinly
overspread with savage flocks, which starvingly support
as savage inhabitants. My last stage was Inveraray[2]—
tomorrow night's stage, Dumbarton.[3] I ought sooner to
have answered your kind letter, but you know I am a
man of many sins . . . the Devil's Day-book only April 14
or fifteenth so cannot yet have increased her growth
much. I began, from that, and some other circumstances,
to suspect foul play; and to tell the truth I w . . .[4]

It is unlikely that the latter and now lost portion of the letter
had any further relevance to the tour, which was later
described by W. E. Henley as 'largely an occasion to drink
and talk'. His 'Devil's Day-book' reckoning referred to May
Cameron's illegitimate child, the result of his recent Edinburgh
fornication.[5]
    Burns's visit to Inveraray was not a happy one, as is seen
from his epigrammatic squib:

> *Whoe'er he be that sojourns here,*
>   *I pity much his case,*
> *Unless he come to wait upon*
>   *The Lord their God, his Grace.*
>
> *There's naething here but Highland pride,*
>   *And Highland scab and hunger;*
> *If Providence has sent me here,*
>   *'Twas surely in an anger.*

These lines were published in Stewart's *Poems Ascribed to
Robert Burns* (1801) with notes to the effect that Burns's
epigram was occasioned by the fact that the Duke of Argyll,
the 5th Duke John Campbell (1723–1806), was holding a large
house party at the time. Apparently the innkeeper was too

busy attending to the Duke's guests to have time to satis-
factorily serve Burns. In the Stewart & Meikle tracts (first
issued 26 July 1799), another set of lines was printed, 'said to
have been inscribed by Burns on a pane of glass in a Highland
Inn':

Highland pride, Highland scab, Highland hunger,
If God Almighty sent me here, 'twas surely in his anger.

As William Ernest Henley and Thomas F. Henderson pointed
out in their *The Poetry of Robert Burns* (London: T. C. & E. C.
Jack, 1896–97, Vol. II), 'It may be that these were the lines
inscribed at Inveraray and that the version in the text has
been elaborated from them.'[6]

While in Tarbet Burns is thought to have written a poem
on the innkeeper's daughter Miss McLauchlan, but the holograph has been lost.

Two other pieces of documentation show that the rest of his
journey was happier. The first is the Dumbarton Burgess
Ticket presented to Burns on 29 June 1787, made out and
signed by the Town Clerk, John McAulay, who entertained
the poet at his home, Levengrove House, where Burns may
possibly have stayed.[7] The ticket, which now hangs in the
Dumbarton Municipal Buildings, declares that 'At Dumbarton, the twenty-ninth day of June, seventeen hundred and
eighty-seven. In the Presence of James Colquhoun of New-
lands, esquire, Provost of the Burgh of Dumbarton[8]; Neil
Campbell[9] and Robert Gardner, esquires, Bailies; Robert
McLintock, Dean of Guild; and John Jarden, Treasurer thereof
compeared Mr Robert Burns of Ayrshire, who was admitted
and received an Burgess and Guild Brother of the said burgh,
with the power to him to use and enjoy all the privileges and
immunities thereto belonging. Extracted by John McAulay.'

The ticket was presented to Dumbarton on 29 June 1926 by
Mrs Violet Burns Gowring, a great-granddaughter of the poet.
To commemorate the event, Ian Strang was commissioned to
prepare an etching of the poet and the Burgess ticket.

It is likely that Burns met the magistrates and received his ticket in the Tolbooth (demolished 1830), which Robert MacFarlan remarks 'stood on the site of Heggie's Buildings, opposite the Elephant and Castle [the Town Arms Hotel]'. Likewise it is probable that Burns made a visit to the now long defunct 'Kings Arms' in the High Street (the site is now occupied by Messrs Burton; Freeman, Easifit).

Burns was obviously well pleased with his reception in Dumbarton and with McAulay's hospitality. In a letter to the Town Clerk dated 4 June 1789, from Ellisland (printed by Currie in 1800: MS. not traced), Burns has this to say: 'There is a certain pretty large quantum of kindness for which I remain, and from inability I fear must remain, your debtor; but though unable to repay the debt, I assure you, Sir, I shall ever warmly remember the obligation.'

According to a nineteenth-century tradition, Burns's name does not appear on the Dumbarton Burgh Roll because of the opposition to his acceptance as a freeman by the extreme Calvinist parish minister, the Rev. James Oliphant (1734–1818), the famous 'Auld Lichter'; he had been the evangelical minister of Kilmarnock High Church, 1764–73. Oliphant had incurred the satire of Burns who in his 1786 poem 'The Ordination' had lambasted the priest for hypocrisy. It must be remembered, however, that there was a certain amount of laxity in the admission and recording of honorary burgesses in Dumbarton (and elsewhere) in the eighteenth century; a factor noted by Fergus Roberts in his *Roll of Dumbarton Burgesses and Guild-Brethren*.

Incidentally, when Robert MacFarlan wrote his short monograph, he cited the 'Arrochar' letter of 25 June 1787 as 'supporting another tradition to the effect that Burns . . . visited the Freemasons' Lodge and was made an honorary member . . .' Again there is no documentary evidence to support this.

The second document of his tour hereabouts is a lively account of the poet's progress down Loch Lomondside which Burns penned as part of the letter to James Smith (1765–

c. 1823), the rabelaisian draper of Mauchline, who was then at Linlithgow:

Burns's Highland Misadventure, 30 June 1787

On our return, at a Highland gentleman's hospitable mansion, we fell in with a merry party, and danced till the ladies left us, at three in the morning. Our dancing was none of the French or English insipid formal movements; the ladies sung Scotch songs like angels, at intervals; then we flew at Bab the Bowster,[10] Tullochgorum, Loch Errol Side, &c, like midges*ᵃ* sporting in the mottie*ᵇ* sun, or craws*ᶜ* prognosticating a storm in a hairst*ᵈ* day. When the dear lasses left us, we ranged round the bowl till the good-fellow hour of six; except a few minutes that we went out to pay our devotions to the glorious lamp of day peering over the towering top of Benlomond. We all kneeled; our worthy landlord's son held the bowl; each man a full glass in his hand; and I, as priest, repeated some rhyming nonsense, like Thomas-a-Rhymer's prophicies I suppose. After a small refreshment of the gifts of Somnus, we proceeded to spend the day on Lochlomond, and reached Dumbarton in the evening. We dined at another good fellow's house, and consequently, pushed the bottle; when we went out to mount our horses, we found ourselves 'No vera fou*ᵉ* but gaylie yet'. My two friends and I rode soberly down the Loch side, till by came a Highlandman at the gallop, on a tolerably good horse, but which had never known the ornaments of iron or leather. We scorned to be outgalloped by a Highlandman, so off we started, whip and spur. My companions, though seemingly gaily mounted, fell sadly astern; but my old mare, Jenny Geddes, one of the Rosinante[11] family, strained past the Highlandman in spite of all his efforts with the hair halter; just as I was passing him, Donald wheeled his horse, as if to cross before me to mar my progress, when down came his

---

ᵃ mosquitoes ᵇ crows ᶜ dusty ᵈ harvest ᵉ drunk

horse, and threw his rider's breekless a[rs]e in a clipt
hedge; and down came Jenny Geddes over all, and my
Bardship between her and the Highlandman's horse.
Jenny Geddes trode over me with such cautious rever-
ence, that matters were not so bad as might well have
been expected; so I came off with a few cuts and bruises,
and a thorough resolution to be a pattern of sobriety in
future . . .[12]

Allan Bayne suggested (*Burns Chronicle*, 1906) convincingly
that Burns's two companions were probably Major William
Colquhoun, son of Sir James Colquhoun (1714–86) of Rosedow,
and Tobias George Smollett, grandson of Commissary James
Smollett (d. 1775) of Cameron House, the 'Highland gentleman's hospitable mansion'.

By 2 July 1787 Burns was again in Mauchline, having
passed through Paisley on his way from Dumbarton.[13]

Notes

1. *Mary Campbell* (1763–86): daughter of Archibald Campbell of Daling, seaman. In her early days she was a nursemaid at the house of Gavin Hamilton in Mauchline. After that she became a dairymaid at Coilsfield. It is not known where Burns first met her, but it was probably around March 1786. A historic theory backed up by the research of Dr F. B. Snyder and Hilton Brown (*There was a Lad*, London: Hamish Hamilton, 1949) suggests that Burns and Mary Campbell had a full sexual relationship, which may have led to her death in childbirth.

2. Royal and municipal burgh and county town of Argyllshire. Famous for its ducal mansion, Inveraray Castle, chief seat of the Dukes of Argyll. The original castle was built in the fifteenth century as the stronghold of the first Earl of Argyll, head of the clan Campbell. The present castle was built in 1744 and was laid out by Archibald, the 3rd Duke. (Plate 4.)

3. A royal burgh on the Clyde, formerly the ancient capital of Strathclyde. (Plate 5.)

4. James Currie published the first paragraph of this letter in 1800. In the Scottish National Portrait Gallery at Edinburgh there is a fragment of this letter with the date and salutation on one side, and the concluding lines on the other, which were first collected for publication by J. de Lancey Ferguson in 1931. Ferguson confirmed that the remainder of the letter was lost.

5. See: Brown, Raymond Lamont, *Clarinda: The Intimate Story of Robert Burns and Agnes Maclehose*, p. 53.

6. The third extant variations printed and published by the Rev. P. Hately Waddell (1867) are probably owing to the bad memory of his informant, Dr James Grierson, who, it appears, fell in with Burns during the journey.

7. Both Robert Rodger and James L. Hempstead categorically state that Burns stayed at Levengrove House, but this has never been authenticated by documentary evidence.

8. Provost, 1783–89, Master of the Freemasons Lodge 1777–84.

9. He acted as cicerone to Dr Samuel Johnson and James

Boswell on their visit to Dumbarton Castle, 28 October 1773; he was related by marriage to the Rev. James Oliphant.

10. These are a representative collection of old Scottish dances. 'Bab the Bowster' was a particular favourite at 'penny weddings' and rustic dances alike. As practised in this part of Scotland in Burns's time, 'Bab the Bowster' was a lengthy dance: A row of men and a row of women faced each other, with one in the middle carrying a bolster. The company sang: 'Wha learnt you to dance, you to dance, you to dance, Wha learnt you to dance, Bab at the Bowster brawly.' At the end of each stanza, the bolster holder laid it at the feet of one of the women and then both knelt for a kiss; the process was then repeated. (See: *The Songs of Robert Burns*. Ed. J. C. Dick, London, 1903.)

11. An allusion to the horse of Don Quixote.

12. De Lancey Ferguson records that this letter was quoted by Currie in 1803, but the holograph cannot be traced. Burns also mentions the race in a letter to John Richmond (1765–1846) from Mossgiel, 7 July 1787.

13. Projected outward route: Glasgow, Dumbarton, Barrachra, Luss, Arrochar, Tarbert, Inveraray. Probable homeward route would include: Inveraray, Arrochar, Luss, Loch Lomond, Dumbarton, Glasgow, Paisley, Kilmarnock, Mauchline. cf. McNaught, D. *The Truth About Burns* (Glasgow: Maclehose & Jackson, 1901).

The Highland Tour with William Nicol

Between his tour of the Western Highlands and his junket with William Nicol, Robert Burns continued his love affair with his future wife Jean Armour (1767–1834), and wrote his famous autobiographical letter to Dr John Moore. By 7 August 1787, Burns had returned to Edinburgh and was mainly concerned while in the capital with prising royalties out of his miserly publisher William Creech (1745–1815); and, of course, with the arrangements for his projected tour of the Highlands.

Burns's choice of William Nicol as a travelling companion is not as strange as it may at first seem; and may very well have been a deliberate snub by Burns on the Edinburgh 'gentry', who treated him so patronisingly. Nicol had been born at Dumbretton, in the parish of Annan, in 1744, the son of a tailor. A man of great talent and ability, Nicol had studied at Edinburgh University and at the time of his first meeting with Burns was classical master at the High School at Edinburgh. In his *Memorials of his Time*, Henry Lord Cockburn, who had been one of Nicol's pupils, described him thus as a disciplinarian:

> The person to whose uncontrolled discipline I was now subjected, though a good man, and intense student and filled, but rather in the memory than in the head, with knowledge, was as bad a schoolmaster as it is possible to fancy. Unacquainted with the nature of youth, ignorant even of the character of his own boys, and with not a conception of the art or of the duty of alluring them, he had nothing for it but to drive them: and this he did by

[13]

constant and indiscriminate harshness. The efforts of this
were very hurtful to all his pupils. Out of the whole four
years of my attendance there were probably not ten days
in which I was not flogged, at least once. The beauty of
no Roman word, or thought, or action ever occurred to
me; nor did I ever fancy that Latin was of any use except
to torture boys.

Nicol was a vain, irascible man and at times a very em-
barrassing friend: indeed Mrs Frances Anna Dunlop (1730–
1815) commented to Burns thus in her letter of November
1790: '[*Nicol*] the world says, has already damned you as an
author.' (Nicol died in 1797 as mutinous as ever.) But it was
probably Nicol's fondness of convivial relaxation which first
attracted Burns to him, even though Burns described his
companionship as being like 'travelling with a loaded blunder-
buss at full cock'.

There are two contemporary accounts of Nicol and Burns
extant, which shed some important and revealing light on
their relationship; and, by inference, the feeling of the upper-
class Edinburgh *literati* towards them. The first account is by
Alexander Young of Harburn, the prim Tory Writer to the
Signet (i.e. lawyer), which appeared in 1834:

> I was just entering into business when Burns came first
> to Edinburgh; and one of my first clients was his friend
> Wm. Nicol, one of the masters of the High School, who
> was the son of a Taylor in the village of Ecclefechan in
> Annandale, employed and patronised by my Grandfather
> and his family; which services were zealously returned to
> me by Mr Nicol in the line of my profession. I considered
> him, and, I believe justly, as one of the greatest Latin
> Scholars of the Age; and when I found him & Burns over
> their Whiskey-punch, (which I had sometimes the honour
> of partaking with them) bandying *extempore* translations
> and imitations of English, Scotch, & Latin Epigrams, I
> could not help considering them as good exemplifications
> of the Italian *Improvisatori* . . . At this time, I looked
> upon Nicol as a far greater Poet and genius than Burns.

He had considerable, indeed constant, employment in translating the Medical & Law Theses of the graduates at the University, for which he made liberal charges, but was very ill paid. I was employed by him to recover many of these claims from English students, concerning which I corresponded with the late Mr [*William*] Roscoe (then an Attorney in Liverpool); and on communicating to Nicol some of Mr Roscoe's letters signifying that several of his claims were considered to be doubtful, if not desperate, he fell into an extravagant rage, swore the most unseemly oaths & uttered the grossest blasphemies, that 'if our Saviour were again on Earth and had employed him to translate a Thesis without paying him for it, he would crucify Him over again'. In consequence of these and similar exhibitions, I thought it prudent to detach myself from such companions; but I never had any quarrel with them.

This quote is an extract from the memoirs now known as the 'Young Manuscript', which is to be found in the library of the University of Edinburgh. The second Nicol–Burns pen portrait was prepared by the Rt Hon. Charles Hope (later Lord Granton):

I met Burns several times at dinner in different Houses, when he first came to Edinr but I was not at all intimate with him. That visit of his to Edinr was a great misfortune to him, & led to all his after follies & misconduct, & ultimately to his ruin & premature death—to all of which his intimacy with Nicol mainly contributed— Nicol . . . was a good scholar; but I did not consider him as a *better* scholar than Adam* or Fraser†—His passions were quite ungovernable, & he was altogether a most ungovernable savage—He persecuted poor Adam by every means in his power; & at least was guilty of a brutal assault on him . . .

* *Dr Alexander Adam* (*1741–1806*), Rector of the High School. Burns had a poor opinion of him.
† *Luke Fraser*, Latin master at the High School.

Nicol thus was universally disliked in Edinburgh, and although Lord Granton overestimates the damage done to Burns's reputation through his friendship with Nicol, the quarrelsome schoolmaster did cause Burns social embarrassment.

On 23 August 1787 Burns wrote to Robert Ainslie at Berrywell House, Duns, Berwickshire, that Nicol had suggested they tour the Highlands in a chaise: 'to which I say, Amen' added Burns. This time historians and researchers can follow the tour in contemporary itinerary, for Burns wrote up the tour as a journal.

This 'journal', however, appears to have been transcribed and extended by Burns at some date later than 1789. We know that this 'extended journal' came into the hands of Sir Walter Scott's son-in-law, James Gibson Lockhart (1794–1854), while he was preparing his regrettable *Life of Robert Burns* (Constable, 1828). Lockhart published 'some fragments', but it was afterwards published more fully (but for some reason not *in extenso*) by Allan Cunningham (1784–1842) in his treacherous *The Works of Robert Burns, with his Life* (London, 1834).

The portions of the holograph manuscript 'journal' set out below in square brackets do not appear in the *original* journal, but have been built up conjointly from the manuscript in the Burns Cottage Museum, and the texts of the 'fragments' noted by J. G. Lockhart and Allan Cunningham and the facsimile edition of J. C. Ewing (1927).

Robert Burns's Journal of his Tour in the Highlands

                              Edinr, the 25th Aug: 1787
I set out for the north in company with my good friend Mr N[icol whose originality of humour promises me much entertainment]; from Corstorphine[13] by Kirkliston[14] and Winsburg,[15] fine, improven, fertile country; near Linlithgow the land's worse; light and sandy. [The more elegant and luxury among the farmers, I always observe, in equal proportion the rudeness and stupidity of the peasantry. This remark

I have made all over the Lothians, Merse, Roxburgh, &c. For this, among other reasons, I think that a man of romantic taste, a 'Man of Feeling',[16] will be better pleased with the poverty, but intelligent minds, of the peasantry in Ayrshire (peasantry they are, all below the Justice of Peace) than the opulence of a club of Merse farmers, when at the same time he considers the vandalism of their plough-folks, &c. I carry this idea so far that an uninclosed, half-proven country is to me actually more agreeable, and gives me more pleasure as a prospect, than a country cultivated like a garden.] Linlithgow,[17] the appearance of rude, decayed, idle grandeur—charmingly rural, retired situation—the old royal palace a tolerably fine, but melancholy, ruin—sweetly situated on a small elevation by the brink of a Loch—shown the room where the beautiful injured Mary Queen of Scots was born—a pretty good old Gothic church—the infamous stool of repentance[18] standing, in the old Romish way, on a lofty situation.

What a poor, pimping business is a Presbyterian place of worship, dirty, narrow and squalid, stuck in a corner of old Popish grandeur such as Linlithgow and, much more, Melrose! ceremony and show, if judiciously thrown in, absolutely necessary for the bulk of mankind, both in religious and civil matters.—Dine.—Go to my friend Smith's[19] at Avon print-field—find nobody but Mrs Miller, an agreeable, sensible, modest, good body; as useful, but not so ornamental, as Fielding's Miss Western[20] not rigidly polite *à la françuis*, but easy, hospitable, and housewifely—An old lady from Paisley, a Mrs Lawson [from *deleted*] whom I promise to call for in Paisley—like old Lady W[*auchope*][21] and still more like Mrs C[*ockburn*][22], [she *deleted*] her conversation is pregnant with strong sense and just remark, but, like them, a certain air of self-importance and a *duresse* in the eye seem to indicate, as the Ayrshire wife observ'd of her cow, that 'She had a mind o' her ain'.[23]

Pleasant view of Dunfermline[24] and the rest of the fertile coast of Fife, as we go down to that dirty, ugly place, Borrowstounness[25]—see a horse-race and call at a friend of Mr Nicol's,

a Bailie Cowan,[26] of whom I know too little to attempt his
portrait—Come through the rich Carse of Falkirk to Falkirk[27]
to pass the night.

[Sunday, 26 August]—Falkirk nothing remarkable except the
tomb of Sir John of Graham, over which, in the succession of
time, has [had *deleted*] been four stones laid. Camelon,[28] the
ancient Metropolis of the Picts, now a small village in the
neighbourhood of Falkirk—Cross the grand canal to Carron[29]
—breakfast—Come past Larbert[30] and admire a fine monu-
ment of cast iron by Mr Bruce,[31] the African traveller, to his
wife. N.B.—he used her very ill, and I suppose he meant it
as much out of gratitude to Heaven as any thing else—
Pass Dunipace,[32] a place laid out with fine taste—a charming
amphitheatre bounded by Denny village,[33] the pleasant seats
of Herbertshire,[34] Denovan[35] and down the way to Dunipace
—The Carron running down the bosom of the whole makes it
one of the most charming little prospects I have seen—dine
at Auchenbowie[36]—Mr Monro[37] an excellent, worthy, old
man—
Miss Monro an amiable, sensible, sweet young woman, much
resembling Mrs Grierson[38]—Come on to Bannockburn[39]—
shown the old house where James 3d was murdered—the field
of Bannockburn—the hole where glorious Bruce set his standard. [Here no Scot can pass uninterested.—I fancy to myself
that I see my gallant, heroic countryman coming o'er the hill
and down upon the plunderers of their country, the murderers
of their fathers; noble revenge and just hate glowing in every
vein, striding more and more eagerly as they approach the
oppressive, insulting, blood-thirsty foe! I see them meet in
gloriously-triumphant congratulation on the victorious field,
exulting in their heroic royal leader and rescued liberty and
independence!]—Come to Stirling[40]—
[Monday, 27 August]—go to Harvieston—Mrs Hamilton[41] and
family, Mrs Chalmers, Mrs Shields[42]—go to see Caldron Linn
and rumbling-bridge and deil's mill[43]—return in the evening
—Supper—Messrs Doig, the Schoolmaster,[44] Bell,[45] and
Captain Forrester of the Castle[46]—D[*oig*], a queerish fellow,

and something of a pedant—B[*ell*] a joyous, vacant fellow, who sings a good song—Forrester a merry, swearing kind of man, with a dash of the Sodger.

[Tuesday, 28 August] morning—breakfast with Captain Forrester—Ochel Hills[47]—Devon river[48]—Forth and Tieth[49] —Allan river[50]—Strathallan[51] a fine country, but little improved—Ardoch camp[52]—cross Earn of Crief[53]—dine, and go to Aberuchil[54]—cold reception at Aberuchil—a most romanticly pleasant ride up Earn, by Auchtertyre[55] and Comrie[56] to Aberuchil—sup at Crieff.

[Wednesday, 29 August] morning—leave Crieff—Glen Aumond[57]—Aumond river—Ossian's grave[58]—Loch Fruoch[59]— Glenquaich[60]—landlord and landlady remarkable characters —Taymouth[61]—described in rhyme—Meet the hon. Charles Townsend.[62]

[Thursday, 30 August] Wednesday [*sic: error in Burns's dating*]—come down Tay to Dunkeld[63]—Glenlyon house[64]— Lyon river—Druid's temple—3 circles of stones—the outmost sunk—the 2d has 13 stones remaining—the innermost has 8 —two large detached ones like a gate, to the southeast—say prayers in it—Pass Tay bridge[65]—Aberfeldy[66]—described in rhyme—Castle Menzies[67]—Grantully[68]—Ballechin beyond[69] —Loggierait[70]—Inver[71]—Dr Stewart[72]—sup.

[Friday, 31 August]—breakfast [*deleted*] walk with Mrs Stewart and Beard[73] to Birnam top[74]—fine prospect down Tay—Craigiebarns hills[75]—hermitage on the Bran water,[76] with a picture of Ossian—Breakfast with Dr Stuart[77]—Neil Gow plays—a short, stout-built, honest highland figure, with his grayish hair shed on his honest social brow—an interesting face, marking strong sense, kind open-heartedness mixed with unmistrusting simplicity—visit his house—Marget Gow.[78]

Friday—ride up Tummel river to Blair[79]—Fascally,[80] a beautiful romantic nest—wild grandeur of the pass of Gilliecrankie[81]—visit the gallant Lord Dundee's stone.

Blair—sup with the Duchess[82]—easy and happy from the manners of the family—confirmed in my good opinion of my friend Walker.[83]

C

[Saturday, 1 September]—visit the scenes round Blair—fine, but spoilt with bad taste—Tilt and Garrie rivers[84]—falls on the Tilt—heather seat—ride in company with Sir William Murray[85] and Mr Walker to Loch Tummel—meanderings of the Rannoch [read, *Tummel*], which runs through quondam Struan-Robertson's estate[86] from Loch Rannoch to Loch Tummel—Dine at Blair—Company—General Murray,[87] *rien* —Captain Murray,[88] an honest Tar—Sir W. Murray, an honest, worthy man, but tormented with the hypochondria —Mrs Graham,[89] *belle et aimable*—Miss Cathcart[90]—Mrs Murray,[91] a painter—Mrs King[92]—Duchess and fine family, the Marquis, Lords James, Edward and Robert[93]—Ladies, Charlotte, Emelia and [Elizabeth][94]—children dance—sup— Duke[95]—Mr Graham of [Fin *deleted*] Fintray[96]—Mr Mlaggan,[97] Mr and Mrs Stewart.[98]

[*There appears to be some half a dozen lines in Burns's hand here, but the pencil is badly smudged. In the decipherable part Burns seems to be mentioning Badenoch, with a note about one Ruthven of Badenoch, all of which he mentions again below. This is followed by the transposed 'Aviemore' paragraph; this has been put right in the following text.*]

[Sunday, 2 September]—Come up the Garrie—falls of Bruar[99] —Daldecairoch[100]—Dalwhinnie[101]—dine—snow on the hills 17 feet deep—no corn from Loch Garrie to Dalwhinnie— Cross the Spey[102] and come down stream to Pitnim[103]— Straths rich—*les environs* picturesque—Craigow hill[104]— Ruthven of Badenoch[105]—barracks—wild and magnificent— Rothemurchie[106] on the other side, and Glenmore[107]—Grant of Rothemurchie's poetry[108] told me by the Duke of Gordon —Strathspey rich and romantic.

[Monday, 3 September]—breakfast at Aviemore,[109] a wild romantic spot—Snows in patches on the hills 18 feet deep— enter Strathspey[110]—come to Sir James Grant's[111]—dine— company—Lady Grant a sweet, pleasant body—Mr and Miss Bailie,[112] Mrs Bailie, Dr and Mrs Grant,[113] Clergymen—Mr Hepburn[114]—come thro' mist and darkness to Dulsie,[115] to lie.

[Tuesday, 4 September]—Findhorn river[116]—rocky banks—

come on to Castle Cawdor[117]—where Macbeth murdered King
Duncan—Saw the bed in which King Duncan was stabbed
—Dine at Kilbraick[118]—Mrs Rose,[119] Senr, a true Chieftain's
wife, a daughter of Clephane—Mrs Rose,[120] Jun—Fort
George[121]—Inverness.[122]

[Wednesday, 5 September]—Loch Ness[123]—Braes of Ness—
General's hut[124]—Falls of Foyers[125]—Urquhart Castle[126] and
Strath—Dine at [*Burns left this entry blank*]—Sup at Mr
Inglis's; Mr Inglis, Mrs Inglis, three young ladies.[127]

[Thursday, 6 September]—Come over Culloden Muir—reflections on the field of battle[128]—breakfast at Kilraick[129]—
Old Mrs Rose, sterling sense, warm heart, strong passions
—and honest pride, all in an uncommon degree—Mrs Rose,
Junr, a little milder than the Mother, this perhaps owing to
her being younger—Mr Grant, minister at Calder, resembles
Mr Scott at Inverleithing [read, *Innerleithen*[130]]—Mrs R[*ose*]
and M. Grant accompany us to Kildrumie[131]—two young
ladies—Miss Ross[132] who sang two Gallic [read, *Gaelic*] songs,
beautiful and lovely—Miss Sophie Brodie,[133] not very beautiful but most agreeable and amiable—both of them the
gentlest, mildest, sweetest creatures on earth, and happiness
be with them—dine at Nairn[134]—Fall in with a pleasant
enough gentleman, Dr Stewart,[135] who had been long abroad
with his father in [*consequence of*] the forty-five, and Mr
Falconer[136] a spare, irascible, warm-hearted Norland, and a
nonjuror—wastes of sand—Brodie house to lie—Mr Brodie
truly polite, but not just the highlander's cordiality.

[Friday, 7 September]—cross the Findhorn to Forres[137]—
Famous stone at Forres—Mr Brodie tells me that the muir
where Shakespeare lays Macbeth's witch meeting is still
haunted—that the country folks won't pass it by night—
Elgin[138] to breakfast; meet with Mr [*Burns left this entry
blank*], Mr Dunbar's friend,[139] a pleasant sort of man; can
come no nearer—venerable ruins of Elgin Abbey—a grandeur
effect at first glance than Melrose, but nothing near so beautiful—cross Spey to Fochabers[140]—fine palace,[141] worthy of the
noble, the polite, the generous Proprietor—Dine—Company,

Duke and Duchess, Ladies Charlotte and Madelina, Colonel Abercrombie and lady,[142] Mr Gordon and Mr [*Burns left this entry blank*],[143] a clergyman, a venerable aged figure, and Mr Hoy,[144] a clergyman, I suppose, a pleasant, open manner —The Duke makes me happier than ever great man did— noble, princely, yet mild, condescending and affable, gay and kind—The Duchess charming, witty, kind and sensible—God bless them! Come to Cullen[145] to lie—hitherto the country is sadly poor and unimproven, the houses, crops, horses, cattle, etc., all in unison—[*with there, deleted*] cartwheels with low, coarse, unshod, clumsy work: an axletree which had been made with other design than to be a resting shaft between the wheels.

[Saturday, 8 September]—Breakfast at Banff[146]—improvements over this part of the country—plenty turnips, wheat, house-hold kail, cabbage, &c. [Portsoy Bay[147]—Duff House[148] —sand-end—and very high—lime plenty—turnips, wheat, household kail, cabbages, etc.: *this portion scored out by steel nibbed pen, but not apparently by Burns*]—pleasant ride along the shore—country almost wild again between Banff and Newbyth[149]—quite wild as we come thro' Buchan to Old Dear,[150] but near the village both lands and crops rich—lie Saturday.

[Sunday, 9 September]—Set out for Peterhead[151]—near Peterhead [the way *deleted*] come along the shore by the famous Bullers of Buchan and Blains Castle[152]—the soil rich—crops of wheat, turnips, etc., but no inclosing—soil rather light— come to Ellan[153] and dine—Lord Aberdeen's seat—entrance denied to everybody, owing to the jealousy of three-score over a kept country-wench—soil and improvements as before till we come to Aberdeen to lie.[154]

[Monday, 10 September]—meet with Mr Chalmers,[155] Printer, a facetious fellow—Mr Ross, a fine fellow, like Professor Tytler;[156] Mr Marshall,[157] one of the *poetae minores*; Mr Sheriffs,[158] author of 'Jamie and Bess', a little decrepid body, with some abilities; Bishop Skinner,[159] a non-juror, son of the author of 'Tullochgorum', a man whose mild, venerable

manner is the most marked of any in so young a man—
Professor Gordon,[160] a good-natured, jolly-looking professor
—Aberdeen a lazy town—near Stonehaven[161] the coast a good
deal romantic—meet my relations—Robert Burnes, writer in
Stonehaven, one of those who love fun, a gill, a punning joke,
and have not a bad heart—his wife a sweet hospitable body,
without any affectation of what is called town breeding.[162]
[Tuesday, 11 September]—Breakfast with Mr Burnes—lie at
Laurencekirk[163]—Album—Library—Mrs [*Burns left this entry
blank*], a jolly, frank, sensible, love-inspiring widow—Howe of
the Mearns,[164] a rich, cultivated, but still uninclosed, country.
[Wednesday, 12 September]—Cross North Esk river and a
rich country, to Craigo.[165] Go to Montrose, that finely-
situated handsome town . . .
[Thursday, 13 September]—Leave Montrose—breakfast at
Auchmithie,[166] and sail along that wild rocky coast, and see the
[famous] Caverns, particularly ye Garriepot[167]—land and dine
at Arbroath[168]—stately ruins Arbroath Abbey—Come to
Dundee,[169] through a fertile Country—Dundee a low-lying but
pleasant town—old steeple—Tayfrith[170]—Broughty Castle,[171]
a finely situated ruin, jutting into the Tay.
[Friday, 14 September]—breakfast with the Miss Scots[172]—
Mr Mitchel[173] an honest Clergyman—Mr Bruce[174] another, but
pleasant, agreeable and engaging—The first from Aberlemno
—the second from Forfar—dine with Mr [Scot *deleted*]
Anderson,[175] a brother-in-law of Miss Scots—Miss Bess Scot
like Mrs Greenfield[176]—my bardship almost in love with her
—come thro' the rich harvests and fine hedge rows of the
carse of Gowrie,[177] along the romantic margin of the Grampian
Hills, to Perth[178]—Castle—Huntly[179]—Sir Stewart Threip-
land.[180]
[Saturday, 15 September]—Perth—Scoon[181]—picture of the
Chevalier and his sister—Queen Mary's bed, the hangings
wrought with her own hands—fine, fruitful, hilly, woody
country round Perth—Tay bridge[182]—Mr and Mrs Hastings[183]
—Major Scot[184]—Castle Gowrie[185]—leave Perth Saturday
morn—come up Strathearn to Endermay[186] to dine—fine,

fruitful cultivated Strath—the scene of 'Bessy Bell and Mary Gray'[187] near Perth—fine scenery on the banks of the May— Mrs Belches,[188] gawcie, frank, affable, fond of rural sports, hunting, &c.—Miss Stirling[189] her sister, *en vérité*—come to Kinross[190] to lie—Reflections in a fit of the Colic.

[Sunday, 16 September]—come through a cold barren Country to Queensferry[191]—dine—cross the Ferry, and come to Edinburgh.

On the day after his arrival at Edinburgh, Robert Burns wrote to his brother Gilbert at Mossgiel with a précis of his tour:

> I arrived here safe yesterday evening after a tour of 22 days, and travelling near 600 miles; windings included.— My farthest stretch was, about 10 miles beyond Inverness.—I went through the heart of the Highlands by Crieff, Taymouth the famous seat of Lord Breadalbine, down the Tay, among cascades & Druidical circles of stones, to Dunkeld seat of the Duke of Athole, thence cross Tay and up one of his tributary streams to Blair of Athole another of the Duke's seats, where I had the honour of spending nearly two days with his Grace and Family, thence many miles through a wild country among cliffs grey with eternal snows and gloomy, savage glens till I crossed Spey and went down the stream through Strathspey so famous in Scottish Music, Badenoch, &c. till I reached Grant Castle, where I spent half a day with Sir James Grant and Family, then cross the country for Fort George—call by the way at Cawdor the ancient seat of McBeth you know in Shakespear, there I saw the identical bed in which Tradition says king Duncan was murdered, lastly from Fort George to Inverness.——
>
> I returned by the coast: Nairn, Forres, and so on to Aberdeen, thence to Stonehive where James Burness from Montrose met me by appointment.—I spent two days among our relatives, and found our aunts, Jean and Isbal still alive and hale old women, John Caird, though

born the same year as our father, walks as vigorously as
I can; they have had several letters from his son in New
York.—William Brand is likewise a stout old fellow: but
further particulars I delay till I see you, which will be in
two or three weeks.

The rest of my stages are not worth rehearsing—
[wa]rm as I was from Ossian's country where I had seen
his very grave, what cared I for fisher-towns and fertile
Carses?—I slept at the famous Brodie of Brodie's one
night and dined at Gordon castle next day with the Duke,
Dutchess and family.*

Overall the pace of his tour was hurried, because of fellow
Jacobite Nicol's impatience. Burns's correspondence of the
period certainly suggests that he would have preferred less
haste. Indeed the poet suggested as much in his letter to
James Hoy of 20 October 1787, with which he enclosed his
song 'Streams that glide in orient plains': 'May that obstinate
son of Latin Prose be curst to Scotch-mile periods, and
damn'd to seven league paragraphs; while Declension &
Conjugation, Gender, Number, and Time, under the ragged
banners of Dissonance and Disarrangement eternally rank
against him in hostile array ! ! ! ! ! !'†

Burns obviously had invitations to present and songs to
collect for James Johnson (c. 1750–1811), editor of the *Scots
Musical Museum*, during the trip, but Nicol remained
difficult. Burns was particularly peeved with Nicol because on
arrival at Fochabers, Burns had left Nicol at the inn, to walk
up to Gordon Castle. There the poet was received warmly and
was pressed to join the company. Burns did join them at
table, but rose soon and said that he must rejoin Nicol.
Whereupon the Duke of Gordon sent a guest with Burns to

---

* This letter was first published by Currie in 1800. De Lancey
Ferguson collected it from a photostat in the Fogg collection,
Main, USA.
† First published Currie 1800. De Lancey Ferguson reported it
as in Gribble collection, Philadelphia.

insist that Nicol return with them to join the party. Nicol,
however, infuriated by the seeming neglect, had ordered the
chaise and blustered that if Burns did not join him immedi-
ately, he would set off alone. Burns joined him, but the
incident rankled with him long after.

The Highland Journal therefore reflects the hurry Burns
was forced into, and preserves the tour in an overall style of
staccato jottings. Therefore the researcher must rely on the
notes of others to fill in much of the background. Bishop
Skinner, for instance, wrote his father a lively account of his
meeting with Burns in Aberdeen; in turn Skinner's father sent
Burns a rhymed epistle which opened a cordial, but brief,
correspondence between them. Bishop Skinner's reflections
and recollections on Burns were as follows:

> Our time was short, as he was just setting off for the south
> and his companion hurrying him; but we had fifty 'auld
> sangs' through hand, and spent an hour or so most
> agreeably.—'Did not your father write the *Ewie wi' the
> crooked horn*?'—'Yes.'—'O, an I had the lown that did
> it !' said he, in a rapture of praise; 'but tell him how I
> love, and esteem, and venerate his truly Scottish muse.'
> On my mentioning *his Ewie*, and how you were delighted
> with it, he said it was all owing to yours, which had
> started the thought. He had been at Gordon Castle, and
> come by Peterhead. 'Then', said I, 'you were within four
> Scottish miles of *Tullochgorum's* dwelling.' Had you seen
> the look he gave, and how expressive of vexation;—had
> he been your own son you could not have wished a better
> proof of affection. 'Well', said he at parting, and shaking
> me by the hand as if he had been really my brother, 'I
> am happy in having seen you, and thereby convey my
> long-harboured sentiments of regard for your worthy sire;
> assure him of it in the heartiest manner, and that never
> did a devotee of the Virgin Mary go to Loretto with more
> fervour than I would have approached his dwelling and
> worshipped at his shrine.' He was collecting on his tour
> the 'auld Scots sangs' he had not before heard of, and
> likewise the tunes that he might get them set to music.

'Perhaps', said he, 'your father might assist me in making this collection; or, if not, I should be happy in any way to rank him among my correspondents.' 'Then give me your direction, and it is probable you may hear from him sometime or other.' On this he wrote his direction on a slip of paper, which I have enclosed that you may see it under his own hand. As to his personal appearance, it is very much in his favour. He is a genteel looking young man of good address, and talks with as much propriety as if he had received an academical education. He has indeed a flow of language, and seems never at a loss to express himself in the strongest and most nervous manner. On my quoting with surprise some sentiments of the Ayrshire *Plowman*, 'Well', said he, 'and a plowman I was from youth, and till within these two years had my shoes studded with a hundred *tackets*. But even then I was a reader, and had very early made all the English poets familiar to me, not forgetting the old bards of the best of all poetical books—the Old Testament.'

Likewise Josiah Walker, the tutor to the Duke of Atholl's household, later recorded his impression of Burns: 'His manner was unembarrassed, plain, and firm. He appeared to have complete reliance on his own native good sense for directing his behaviour. He seemed at once to perceive and to appreciate what was due to the company and to himself, and never to forget a proper respect for the separate species of dignity belonging to each. He did not arrogate conversation, but, when led into it, he spoke with ease, propriety, and manliness. He tried to exert his abilities, because he knew it was ability alone gave him a title to be there. The Duke's fine young family attracted much of his admiration; he drank their healths as *honest men and bonnie lasses*, an idea which was much applauded by the company, and with which he has very felicitously closed his poem.' (See poem in Appendix III.)

Walker also gives us one of the few examples we have of Burns's actual conversation: 'As a specimen of his happiness of conception and strength of expression, I will mention a remark which he made on his fellow-traveller, who was walking, at the time, a few paces before us. He was a man of robust but clumsy person; and while Burns was expressing to me the value he entertained for him, on account of his vigorous talents, although they were clouded at times by coarseness of manners; "in short", he added, "his mind is like his body, he has a confounded strong in-kneed sort of a soul".'

Notes

The Highland Tour with William Nicol

13. *Corstorphine:* Now part of the City of Edinburgh, although it retains its 'village character'; name may mean Cross of Torphine. Famed for its fifteenth-century church, with the tombs of the Lords Forrester. Near the church is a notable seventeenth-century circular dovecote.

14. *Kirkliston:* Village and parish on the River Almond, ten miles west of Edinburgh. Notable church with Norman doorway and saddleback tower. Contains the vault of the first Lady Stair, the original of Lady Ashton in Sir Walter Scott's *The Bride of Lammermoor* (1819).

15. *Winchburgh:* Quoad sacra parish and village in Kirkliston parish; twelve miles west of Edinburgh.

16. *'Man of Feeling':* Allusion to the famous book of the same name published anonymously in 1771 by the novelist and lawyer Henry Mackenzie (1745–1831). His review of Burns's *Poems* in the *Lounger* for 9 December 1786 helped to make the poet's works known amongst the Edinburgh *literati*. (See note 111.)

17. *Linlithgow:* A royal burgh and the county town of West Lothian. Mary Queen of Scots was born at Linlithgow Palace on 7 or 8 December 1542; Prince Charles Edward Stuart was entertained here in 1745. On 3 February 1746 the palace was carelessly burned by the troops of General Henry Hawley (*c.* 1679–1759). Since that time the palace remained a roofless ruin. Beautifully situated with its own loch, the palace was the favourite seat of Scottish monarchs, who held courts and parliaments therein. The palace owed much, including the courtyard fountain, to James V, who was born within its walls. The nearby fifteenth-century church of St Michael was the scene of the 'ghostly figure' affair in which James IV was warned not to invade England. It was in the Palace of Linlithgow, of course, that Sir David Lyndsay's *Satire of the Three Estatis* was first performed in 1540. (Plate 9.)

[29]

According to Dr William Wallace (1843–1921), former editor of
The Glasgow Herald, Burns was made a freeman of Linlithgow on
16 November 1787. But Burns never signed the Burgess Roll, and
there is no independent evidence that Burns was in Linlithgow on
that day, although it is true that he was in Edinburgh. Wallace
claimed that the burgess ticket had been preserved and ran thus:

> At Linlithgow, the sixteenth day of November, one thousand
> seven hundred and eighty seven years, the which day, in the
> presence of James Andrew, Esquire, Provost of the Burgh of
> Linlithgow; William Napier, James Walton, Stephen Mitchell,
> John Gibson, bailies; and Robert Speedie, Dean-of-Guild,
> compeared Mr Robert Burns, Mossgiel, Ayrshire, who was
> made and created Burgess and Guild Brother of the said
> Burgh, having given his oath of fidelity according to the form
> used thereanent.

Andrew McCallum in *Burns Chronicle*, 1944 (page 37), states
that he had traced a 'genuine' ticket which he thought was still in
private hands. The incident remains an academic puzzle.

18. *Stool of repentance:* The famous 'cutty stool'; a short, three-
legged stool, on which sinners sat to be publicly harangued from
the pulpit.

19. *James Smith* (1765–c. 1823): He had a draper's shop in
Mauchline, but subsequently went into partnership with a Linlithgow calico-printer. He later emigrated to Jamaica and died
there. Like Burns an ardent fornicator, Smith was the recipient of
a number of letters from Burns on sex and marriage.

20. Allusion to Henry Fielding's (1707–54) character Sophia
Western in *The History of Tom Jones, A Foundling* (1749).

21. *Lady Wauchope:* Mrs Walter Scott (1729–89), of Wauchope
House, nr Jedburgh, Roxburghshire. (See *Robert Burns's Tour of
the Borders*, p. 33, n. 36.)

22. William Scott Douglas suggests that this person 'may have
been Mrs Cockburn of Crichton St, Edinburgh'. Mrs Alison
Cockburn (1712–94), wife of Patrick Cockburn, authoress of one of
the versions of 'The Flowers of the Forest', was the niece of Mrs
Walter Scott.

23. Translation: 'She had a mind of her own.'

24. *Dunfermline:* A royal burgh in Fife, sixteen miles north-
west of Edinburgh. (See note 201, pp. 57–8.)

25. *Borrowstounness:* Now Bo'ness, burgh of West Lothian,
twenty-one miles from Edinburgh. The Antonine Wall (Graham's
Dyke) traverses the parish.

26. At the time of Burns's visit there were three Cowans—

James, Thomas and Alexander—serving on the Bo'ness Council;
but none appears to have been appointed 'Bailie'. It is possible that
'Bailie' might in fact be the man's Christian name.

27. *Falkirk:* Large burgh eleven miles south-east of Stirling in
East Stirlingshire. Very fertile carse (in Scottish diction, a stretch
of alluvial land along the banks of rivers, etc.) still exists. Hereabouts Edward I defeated Wallace in 1298; in Falkirk churchyard
Stewart of Bute and John de Grahame, the friend of Wallace, are
buried. In his letter of 26 August 1787 from Stirling, to Robert
Muir (1758–88), the Kilmarnock wine-merchant, Burns mentions
kneeling 'at the tomb of Sir John the Graham the gallant friend of
the immortal Wallace' to pray. Here too Prince Charles Edward
defeated General Hawley's troops during his retreat in 1746.
Falkirk was formerly a market town, noted for its Cattle Trysts
(transferred from Crieff in the late eighteenth century). (Plate 10.)
Industry developed with the opening of the Firth & Clyde Canal
in 1790. Burns stayed at the Cross Keys Inn, his room was in the
centre portion of the second floor and here he penned the first
entries in his journal; the site of the inn is now a shop, but a
casting from the Grahamston Foundry with a bust of the poet was
erected in 1889.

Burns is said (by George Boyack, 1792–1854, of St Andrews,
Fifeshire Journal, 4 November 1847) to have scribbled these lines
on the inn window:

> *Sound be his sleep and blithe his morn,*
> *That never did a lassie wrang;*
> *Who poverty ne'er held in scorn*
> *For misery ever tholed a pang.*

Verse not traced.

28. *Camelon:* Quoad sacra parish forming part of Falkirk.
Stands on the site of a Roman town.

29. *Carron:* A village on the River Carron, two miles north-
west of Falkirk. Burns called at the Carron Ironworks which had
been founded by Dr Roebuck of Sheffield in 1759; a works known
for its pieces of artillery (Carronades) used in the Napoleonic wars.
Burns wrote this, with his diamond, on the window of the inn at
Carron (formerly the Carron Company Bank, then tenanted by
William Stewart), because he had been refused entrance to the
works:

> *We cam na here to view your works*
> *In hopes to be mair wise,*
> *But only, lest we gang to hell,*

> *It may be nae surprise:*
> *But when we tirl'd at your door,*
> *Your porter dought na hear us;*
> *Sae may, shou'd we to hell's yetts come,*
> *Your billy Satan sair us!*

An amateur poet called Alexander Benson, who was employed at Carron as Blast Furnace Manager, replied to Burns thus (i.e. referring to Burns's subterfuge):

> *If you came here to see our Works*
> *You should have been more civil*
> *Than give a fictitious name,*
> *In hopes to cheat the Devil.*
> *Six days a week to you and all,*
> *We think it very well;*
> *The other, if you go to church,*
> *May keep you out of Hell.*

30. *Larbet:* Parish and town two and a half miles north-west of Falkirk.

31. *James Bruce* (1730–94): The famous traveller and explorer of the Blue Nile, nicknamed 'Abyssinia' after his exploits. He was married twice; first to Adriana Allen, a Portuguese wine-merchant's daughter, who died in 1754, and secondly to Mary Dundas of Carronhall, who died in 1785.

32. *Dunipace:* Town and parish in East Stirlingshire; noted hills of Dunipace and Dunipace House.

33. *Denny:* Town and parish twelve miles south of Stirling. District rich in Pictish and Roman remains. Ancient Torwood Castle, the formation point in many battles. Sir William Wallace spent his boyhood here.

34. *Herbertshire Castle:* Adjoining Denny. In 1889 it was described (*Castles and Domestic Architecture*, iii, 537 ff) as 'a large and lofty structure. L-shaped on plan, and measuring 63 ft. 6 in. in length, including the wing, by 43 ft. 8 in. in breadth'. It was bought in 1768 by William Moorhead from the Stirlings of Herbertshire. Destroyed by fire in 1914.

35. *Denovan:* House and village, a half mile north of Denny.

36. *Auchinbowie:* Village and seat one and three-quarter miles south-west of Bannockburn. Auchinbowie House stands in its two policies two and a half miles south of the village of St Ninians; the oldest part of the building is an example of a laird's house of the seventeenth century. (Plate 11.)

37. *John Munro* (1725–89): Advocate, son of Dr Alexander Munro (*Primus*), he received the estate of Auchinbowie in 1757. He was a widower at the time of Burns's visit, and his daughter Isabella was as yet unmarried and living at home.

38. Contrary to the opinions of late nineteenth-century Burnsians, this is undoubtedly the spouse of Dr George Grierson, Burns's fellow mason from Glasgow. At this time Burns had not met James Grierson of Dalgoner (1753–1843).

39. *Bannockburn* (Gaelic, 'the stream of the white knoll'): Town in Stirlingshire, on the Bannock Burn, three miles southeast of the town and castle of Stirling. The town of Bannockburn is the scene of Robert the Bruce's victory over the English army of Edward II on 24 June 1314. The 'hole' or 'borestone' mentioned by Burns can still be seen. (Plate 12.)

40. *Stirling:* Royal burgh and county town of Stirlingshire, which dates from Pictish times as a settlement. From the thirteenth to the seventeenth century the castle was the seat of Scottish kings. (Plate 13.) Burns stayed at James Wingate's Inn (Burns's room, third floor, north-east corner), Quality Street, now the Golden Lion Hotel, King Street. Bronze statue of Burns at Stirling by A. H. Hodge, unveiled 23 September 1914. Also 'Hall of Heroes' bust by D. W. Stevenson.

On Sunday, 26 August 1787, Burns is supposed to have written to Robert Muir, '. . . just now, from Stirling Castle, I have seen by the setting sun the glorious prospect of the windings of Forth through the rich carse of Stirling . . .' In this letter he also is said to have noted that he 'said a fervent prayer for Old Caledonia', where Bruce fixed his standard. But as this letter has not been traced in MS., and was first mentioned by Allan Cunningham in 1834, scholars believe the whole to be a fabrication. Likewise there is no documentary evidence to prove the tradition that Burns visited the Stirling Ancient 30 Masonic Lodge.

James Cunningham, fourteenth Earl of Glencairn (1749–91), had given Burns a diamond stylus, and while at Stirling the poet used it to write the following on a window pane, to express his resentment that the old royal palace had been allowed to fall into disrepair:

> *Here Stewarts once in triumph reign'd,*
> *And laws for Scotland's weal ordain'd;*
> *But now unroof'd their Palace stands,*
> *Their sceptre's fall'n to other hands;*
> *Fallen indeed, and to the earth,*
> *Whence grovelling reptiles take their birth.——*
> *The injur'd STEWART-line are gone,*

> *A Race outlandish fill their throne;*
> *An idiot race, to honour lost;*
> *Who know them best despise them most.——*

41. *Mrs Barbara Hamilton:* Second wife of John Hamilton of Kype, a Mauchline lawyer. She moved to Harvieston, near Dollar, the home of the writer John Tait, husband of her sister, on the death of her husband. (See also Appendix II.)

42. *Mrs Euphemia Chalmers:* Second daughter of Thomas Murdoch of Cumloden, who married John Chalmers of Fingland; sister-in-law to John Tait. (See also Appendix II.)

43. *Caldron Linn:* Several waterfalls on River Devon, south-east Perthshire, three miles east of Dollar. *Rumbling Bridge:* On the border of Kinross and Perth shires. Four miles north-east of Dollar. *Devil's Mill:* Cataract on the Devon river, one and a half miles from the Crook of Devon, Kinross. (See also page 53.)

44. *Dr David Doig* (1719–1800): Rector of Stirling Grammar School. A classical and oriental scholar, contributor to *Encyclopaedia Britannica*.

45. *Christopher Bell* (1745–1814): Master of the English School, also music master and precentor of the parish church and later Session Clerk.

46. *Captain Gabriel Forrester* (d. 1813): Actually a lieutenant in Stirling Castle. His mother was Helen Napier, lineal descendant of Sir John Napier of Merchiston, the inventor of logarithms. Burns probably breakfasted with him either at the castle or in Forrester's civilian lodgings.

47. *Ochil Hills:* A range extending some twenty-four miles over parts of Clackmannan, Fife, and Kinross, but chiefly south-east Perthshire. Chief summits: Bencleugh, Dunnyat, King's Seat.

48. *Devon River:* Rises in the southern Ochils, flows through Perthshire, Kinross and Clackmannan shires, enters Forth at Cambus. Burns later wrote the song 'The banks of the Devon' to the tune *Bhannerach dlon na chai*.

49. *Forth and Teith:* Forth rises to the north of Ben Lomond; Teith, east-north-east of the head of Loch Lomond, runs south-east to the Forth.

50. *Allan River:* Affluent of River Forth, rises in the parish of Blackford in the Ochils, enters Forth one and a half miles above Stirling. See the poet's 'Allan Water'.

51. *Strathallan:* Valley of the River Allan.

52. *Ardoch Camp:* A Roman camp in the grounds of Ardoch House, in the Perthshire parish which contains the villages of Braco and Greenloaning.

1 The Archibald Skirving portrait of Robert Burns, 1796–8: based on the bust-portrait by Alexander Nasmyth.

Journal —

Edin[r]. the 25th Aug: 1787, I
set out for the north in company
with my good friend Mr W

[from Edr to Stirling by Kirkaliston
and Winsburg, fine, improven,
fertile country; near Linlithgow
the land's worse; light and sandy.
Linlithgow] the appearance of
rude, decayed, idle grandeur — charmingly rural, retired situation
the old royal palace a tolerably
fine but melancholy ruin —
sweetly situated on a small
elevation by the brink of a

2 Page one of Robert Burns's holograph "Journal" of his Highland
   Tour.

At Dumbarton the Twenty-Ninth day of June Seventeen hundred and Eighty Seven years —

In Presence of James Colquhoun of Nuslands Esquire Provost of the Burgh of Dumbarton Neil Campbell and Robert Gardner Esquires Bailies Robert M'Kintoch Dean of Guild and John Jarden Treasurer thereof Compeared Mr Robert Burns of Ayrshire to his own admitted and received Burgess and Guild Brother of the said Burgh with power to him to use and enjoy all the priviledges and Immunities thereto belonging. Extracted by —

Fortitudo et Fidelitas

Mr. Burns

3 Reduced facsimile of the Dumbarton Burgess Ticket, 1787.

4 Thomas Allom's print of Inveraray Castle.

5 Regency print of the Castle and Town of Dumbarton.

6   The Old Tolbuith of Dumbarton and the Mackenzie House, from George Harcourt's reconstruction 1893.

7   Loch Lomond from the road above Inversnaid Mill, print by Thomas Allom.

8 A. Reid's engraving of Luss House, 1793, the home of Sir James Colquhoun.

9 Linlithgow Palace and parish church.

10 Falkirk.

11 Auchinbowie House, home of John Munro, advocate.

12   The Field of Bannockburn.

13   Stirling Castle.

14   Castle Wynd and Cathedral, Stirling: Burns probably dined here.

15   Aberuchill Castle.

16   D. O. Hill's engraving of Auchtertyre: the estate and house.

17 Kenmore and Taymouth Castle.

18 Thomas Allom's view of Dunkeld.

19   Castle Menzies, home of Sir John Menzies.

20   H. W. William's view of Kilravock Castle.

21　John Murray, 4th Duke of Atholl (1755–1830).

22 W. Richardson's engraving of the Birks of Aberfeldy.

23 Neil Gow, musician (1727–1807).

24 Euphemia Murray,
"The Flower of Strathmore".

25 Bruar Water and Lower Falls

26 Blair Castle, a seat of the Duke of Atholl.

27 Cawdor Castle, Nairnshire.

28   The Pass of Killiecrankie.

29   Ruthven Hanoverian Barracks.

30 Sir James Grant of Grant (1738–1811).

31 Fort George.

32 Inverness, western prospect by Thomas Allom.

33 View of Foyers from above the falls, as Burns saw it.

34 Castle Urquhart and Loch Ness, Inverness-shire.

35 Culloden Moor, Inverness-shire.

36   Brodie Castle.

37   Elgin Cathedral: Thomas Allom's romanticised picture of its destruction in 1390 by the "Wolf of Badenoch", the bloodthirsty son of King Robert II.

38   Castle Gordon, Morayshire, seat of the Duke of Gordon.

39   Auchmithie, Angus.

Plate 66

DUFF HOUSE, *the Seat of the* EARL *of* FIFE, *in* BAMFSHIRE.

Published according to Act of Parliament by G. Kearsly, in Fleet Street, Novr. 1779.

C. Cordiner *del.*   P. Mazell *sc*

40   Duff House, seat of the Earl of Fife.

41   Peterhead.

42   Arbroath.

43   Montrose.

44 Town and Harbour, Dundee, 1793.

45 The River Devon at the Rumbling Bridge.

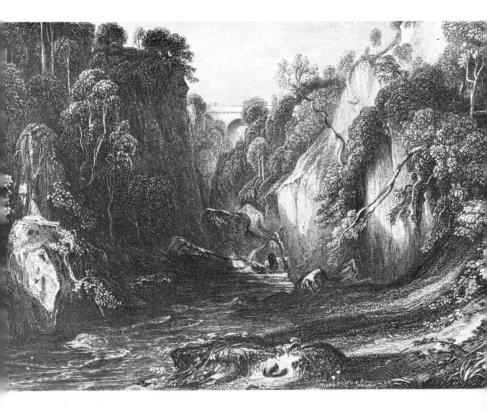

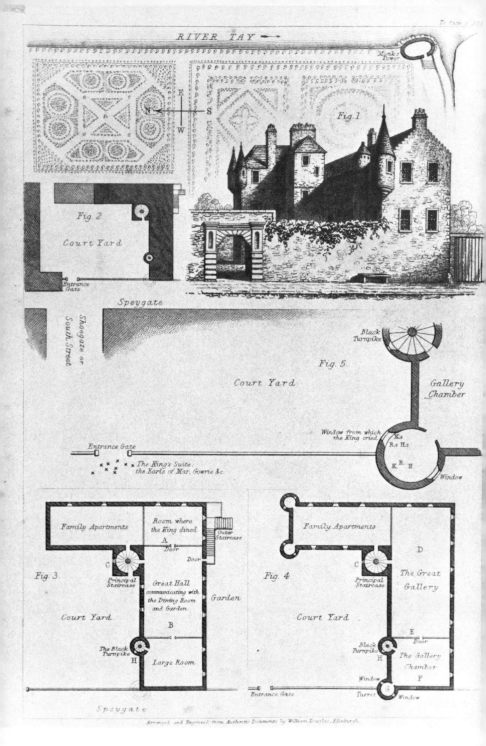

To face p. 326

RIVER TAY →

E
N ← S
W

Fig. 1.

Monks Tower

Fig. 2
Court Yard

Entrance Gate

Speygate

Shoegate or South Street

Fig. 5.

Black Turnpike

Court Yard

Gallery Chamber

Window from which the King cried

K.s R.s H.s

K R. H

Window

Entrance Gate

× × × ×
× × ×
The King's Suite;
the Earls of Mar, Gowrie &c.

Family Apartments

Room where the King dined

A
Door

Outer Staircase

Door

Fig. 3.

C
Principal Staircase

Great Hall communicating with the Dining Room and Garden

Garden

Court Yard

B

The Black Turnpike

H

Large Room

Speygate

Family Apartments

C
Principal Staircase

D

Fig. 4.

The Great Gallery

Court Yard

E
Door

Black Turnpike

H

The Gallery Chamber

F

Window

Entrance Gate

Turret

G

Window

Arranged and Engraved from Authentic Documents by William Douglas, Edinburgh.

46 Gowrie House, Perth. Demolished 1807. Print shows details of the Gowrie Conspiracy.

47   Harvieston Castle, home of John Tait, advocate.

48   Hogg's Print of Dunfermline Abbey in Burns's day.

49 Mrs. Catherine Bruce
(1696–1791) at the age of

50 Margaret Chalmers
drawn by J. Irvine.

53. *Crieff:* Town and parish of Perthshire above the River Earn.

54. *Aberuchill:* An estate with mansion house, remains of an old castle, one and three-quarter miles south-west of Comrie. (Plate 15.)

55. *Ochtertyre:* An estate with house, three miles north-west of Crieff. (Plate 16.)

56. *Comrie:* Parish and town of Perthshire.

57. *Glenalmond:* Four miles north-west of Methuen on the River Almond, a tributary of the Tay.

58. *Ossian's Grave:* A large stone, near the River Almond, six miles north-east of Crieff.

59. *Loch Freuchie:* Loch north of the quoad sacra parish and village of Amulrie, twelve miles north-east of Crieff. Here the clans were armed and sworn in at the 1715 rising.

60. *Glen Quaich:* Six miles south of Aberfeldy, Perthshire, on the River Quaich, which flows into the head of Loch Freuchie.

61. *Taymouth:* Seat of John Campbell (1762-1834), one of the sixteen Scottish representative peers; created Baron Breadalbane of Taymouth Castle in 1806. Marquis in 1831. Burns prefaced his 'Address to Beelzebub' to Campbell.

N.B. While at Kenmore, a parish and village on Loch Tay, Burns wrote these lines, in pencil, over the chimney-piece of the inn:

Admiring Nature in her wildest grace,
These northern scenes with weary feet I trace;
O'er many a winding dale and painful steep,
Th'abodes of coveyed grouse and timid sheep,
My savage journey, curious, I pursue,
Till fam'd Breadalbaine opens to my view.——
The meeting cliffs each deep-sunk glen divides,
The woods, wild-scattered, clothe their ample sides;
Th' outstretching lake, imbosomed 'mong the hills,
The eye with wonder and amazement fills;
The Tay meandering sweet in infant pride,
The palace rising on his verdant side;
The lawns wood-fringed in Nature's native taste;
The hillocks dropt in Nature's careless haste;
The arches striding o'er the new-born stream;
The village glittering in the noontide beam——

*   *   *   *   *

Poetic ardours in my bosom swell,
Lone wandering by the hermit's mossy cell:

D

The sweeping theatre of hanging woods;
Th' incessant roar of headlong tumbling floods——

*   *   *   *   *

Here Poesy might wake her heaven taught lyre,
And look through Nature with creative fire;
Here to the wrongs of Fate half reconcil'd,
Misfortune's lightened steps might wander wild;
And Disappointment, in these lonely bounds,
Find balm to soothe her bitter rankling wounds:
Here heart-struck Grief might heavenward stretch her scan,
And injured Worth forget and pardon Man.

Incidentally, it is interesting to note regarding inns hereabouts what R. L. Willis said about them three years after Burns's visit: 'The cheapness of the inns is wonderful. We had today for dinner, fine fresh trout, a shoulder of mutton, two fowls and bacon, hung beef, and salmon salted, vegetables, cheese and an excellent bottle of port; and the sum total was four shillings and twopence.'

    62. *Hon. Charles Townshend* (1728–1810): First Baron Bayning.

    63. *Dunkeld:* Perthshire town, some sixteen miles from Perth. A settlement since the days of Constantine, king of the Picts; town contains the ruins of a cathedral which was founded in 1107, once the seat of Scottish primates. Dunkeld House, a seat of the Duke of Atholl. (See note 79.) (Plate 18.)

    64. *Glenlyon House:* Seat of the Campbells of Glenlyon. Occupied in Burns's day by Dr David Campbell.

    65. *Tay Bridge:* See below.

    66. *Aberfeldy* (Gaelic, *obar Pheallaidh*—confluence of the Peallaidh): On the Tay where it is crossed by one of General George Wade's (1668–1748) finest bridges. (Plate 22.) See the poet's fine lines on the 'Birks':

> *Now Simmer blinks on flowery braes,*
>   *And o'er the chrystal streamlets plays;*
> *Come let us spend the lightsome days*
>   *In the birks of Aberfeldy.——*
>
> *The little birdies blythely sing*
>   *While o'er their heads the hazels hing,*
> *Or lightly flit on wanton wing*
>   *In the birks of Aberfeldy.——*
>
> *The braes ascend like lofty wa's,*
>   *The foamy stream deep-roaring fa's*

O'erhung wi' fragrant-spreading shaws,
The birks of Aberfeldy.——

The hoary cliffs are crown'd wi' flowers,
White o'er the linns the burnie pours
And rising weets wi' misty showers
The birks of Aberfeldy.——

Let Fortune's gifts at random flee,
They ne'er shall draw a wish frae me;
Supreme blest wi' love and thee
In the birks of Aberfeldy.——

Chorus: Bony lassie will ye go, will ye go, will ye go;
Bony lassie will ye go to the birks of Aberfeldy.——

Lines 'Composed on the spot'.

67. *Castle Menzies:* One and a half miles north-west of Aber-feldy. Occupied by Sir John Menzies of Menzies (Chief of the clan Menzies), the fourteenth baronet. The poem 'Theniel Menzies' bony Mary' dates from this period. (Plate 19.)

68. *Grantully:* Also called Grandtully, village on the Tay, two and a half miles north-east of Aberfeldy. Grantully Castle, a fine sixteenth-century baronial mansion. See: 'Tully Veolan' in Sir Walter Scott's *Waverley* (1814).

69. *Ballechin:* Seat in the parish of Logierait, north-central Perthshire. Then occupied by Charles Stuart (or Stewart) of Ballechin, or his son.

70. *Logierait:* Parish and village on the north bank of the Tay, near the influx of the River Tummell.

71. *Inver:* Village, on the right ride of the Tay.

72. *Dr Alexander Stewart:* Medical practitioner originally from Aberfeldy; a connection of Baroness Nairne through marriage, he was known as the Baron of Badenoch. Close friend of the Duke of Atholl.

73. *Beard:* Either a retainer, or a dog? No mention in family histories.

74. *Birnam:* Village on the River Tay, three-quarter mile south-east of Dunkeld. Birnam Top lies between Duncan's Camp (a circular fortification, where King Duncan is said to have held court) and the Tay, and Birnam Pass.

75. *Craigiebarns:* Near Dunkeld; rises to 900 ft.

76. *Bran Water:* Flows from Loch Freuchie to meet the Tay at Dunkeld.

77. *Dr Alexander Stewart:* Burns's misspelling. See note 72.

78. *Neil Gow* (1727–1807): The famous Scots fiddle composer. (Plate 23.) Burns drew many of the airs for his songs from Gow's dance tunes. Gow was born at Inver. (See note 71.) *Margot Gow* (*nee* Wiseman) was the wife of Neil Gow. Local tradition has it that Burns on reaching Dunkeld repaired to Inver Inn with Gow. On seeing and hearing an irate woman, Burns is said to have composed this impromptu verse:

> *Ye gods, ye gave to me a wife,*
> *Out of your grace and pleasure.*
> *To be a partner of my life,*
> *And I was glad to have her.*
>
> *But if your providence divine,*
> *For better things design her,*
> *I obey your will at any time*
> *I'm willing to resign her.*

Scholars believe, however, that the verse is from an old Scots song which Burns may have titivated. (See: T. Davidson Cook, *Weekly Scotsman*, 6 September 1924.)

79. *Blair Castle:* Restored 1872, altered 1903; seat of John Murray, fourth Duke of Atholl. (Plate 26.)

80. *Faskally:* Seat, at the junction of the Tummel and Garry rivers, two miles north-west of Pittochry.

81. *Killiecrankie:* A Pass on the River Garry. At the north end of the Pass the famous battle was fought on 27 July 1689, where John Graham of Claverhouse, Viscount Dundee (b. 1649), defeated the troops of William III under Hugh Mackay (1640–92), and received his death wound. (Plate 28.)

82. *Jane Schaw:* Eldest daughter of the ninth Baron Cathcart, married the fourth Duke on 26 December 1774; she died 4 December 1790.

83. *Josiah Walker* (1761–1831): Youngest son of the Rev. Thomas Walker of Dundonald, Ayrshire. He was tutor (1787) to the Duke of Atholl's son. Walker was introduced to Burns in Edinburgh by Dr Thomas Blacklock (1721–91). Ultimately Walker became Professor of Humanity at Glasgow University.

84. The River *Tilt* issues from Loch Tilt, and flows fifteen miles south-west through Glen Tilt to the River *Garry* at Bridge of Tilt. The River Garry issues from Loch Quaich.

85. *Sir William Murray of Ochtertyre* (d. 1800): See also page 54. NB: Old spelling *Auchtertyre*.

86. *Struan-Robertson:* The Robertsons of Struan were loyal

adherents of the Stuarts. Chief of the clan in Burns's time was Colonel Alexander Robertson.

87. *General Murray:* Burns's vagueness causes some scholastic difficulty here: According to the files in the Public Record Office, there were two Generals by the name of Murray in 1787:

. . . General Sir James Murray, who served in Flanders and Brittany; also at Louisberg and Quebec against the French. Governor of Quebec 1760 and Governor of Canada 1763–66. Governor of Minorca 1774–82. He died around 1794.

. . . Major General James Murray, Colonel of the 72nd (Highland) Regiment in 1787.

88. *Captain Murray:* John, of the Perthshire Murrays; saw service in both crown and merchant fleets; retired from service when Burns met him.

89. *Mrs Graham:* Mary (d. 1792), wife of Sir Thomas Graham (1749–1843), the hero of Barossa.

90. *Louisa, suo jure* Countess of Mansfield (d. 1843). Both Louisa and Mary were sisters to the Duchess.

91. *Mrs Murray:* Euphemia McLean, wife of Captain John Murray. (Note 88).

92. *Mrs King:* Widow. By marriage she was one of the Kings of Newmill, Banffshire.

93. John (1778–1846); James (1782–1837); Edward Murray (1783–95); Robert (1785–93); a fifth son Frederick was born a year after Burns's visit, but died in 1789.

94. Charlotte (1775–1832); Mary Louisa (1776–77); Amelia Sophia (1780–1849); Elizabeth (1787–1846). The Duke was married again in 1794 to Margery, the widow of Lord Macleod.

95. See note 79.

96. *Robert Graham of Fintray* (1749–1815): Late of Forfarshire, Commissioner of the Scottish Board of Excise.

97. *Mr MLaggan:* Thought by Burns researchers to be Henry MacLaggan of Dunavourd, son of the Jacobite William MacLaggan (d. 1767).

98. *David and Elizabeth Stewart of Bonskeid:* As Stewarts of Atholl and kinsmen of the Stewart Earls of Atholl, this couple were related to the Duke of Atholl.

99. *Falls of Bruar:* Bruar water flows into the Garry, three miles west of Blair. (Plate 25.) Whilst Burns was in the area the Duke of Atholl was expecting an important guest, Henry Dundas (1742–1811), William Pitt's political lieutenant for Scotland; and wished to keep Burns as 'the best dainty with which he could entertain an honoured guest'. Burns was pressed by Nicol to move on, but sent this poem a few days later, to pay his 'debts of honour

and gratitude': *The Humble Petition to Bruar Water to the Noble Duke of Athole.* (See Appendix III.)

100. *Dalnacardoch:* A deer forest eleven miles west-north-west of Blair Atholl.

101. *Dalwhinnie:* Glenstruim, thirteen miles south-west of Kingussie.

102. *Spey:* Of one hundred and seven miles in length, the Spey is Scotland's most rapid river; rises five miles from the western side of Loch Luggan.

103. *Pitmain:* Seat one mile south-west of Kingussie.

104. *Craigow hill:* Now unmarked on modern maps.

105. *Ruthven Castle:* The great *motte* of the Norman castle, formerly a stronghold of the Comyns, later of the Gordons, was crowned in Burns's day by the now ruined Hanoverian barracks and garrison buildings, which were a vital link in General Wade's communications system. (Plate 29.)

106. *Rothiemurchus:* Quoad sacra parish, Inverness-shire.

107. *Glenmore:* River and glen, four miles south of Lochalsh.

108. *Grant of Rothiemurchus:* Burns met the Duke of Gordon at Edinburgh in the winter of 1786, and this reference is undoubtedly to this earlier meeting. No references to the poems of Grant have been traced in the standard biographies of Burns, nor has it been possible to trace the publication of the poems in any form. Elizabeth Grant of Rothiemurchus's journals contain some account of the family of Grant of Rothiemurchus, but there is no indication whatsoever that any member of the family was a poet of consequence.

109. *Aviemore:* Twelve and a half miles south-west of Grantown, Inverness.

110. *Strathspey:* Flat valley of the Spey, which rises on the south-east side of Creag a' Chait.

111. *Sir James Grant of Grant* (1738–1811): An office bearer in the Highland Society from 1784. Ultimately a Member of Parliament, Grant was not in the House of Commons during Burns's visit. Burns was introduced to Grant through the latter's brother-in-law, Henry Mackenzie. (Plate 30.)

112. *Col. John Baillie of Dunain:* Officer in the Honourable East India Company; his wife Isabella Campbell and their daughter Catherine (she married Col. Hugh Rose of Kilravock).

113. *Dr Grant:* Untraceable today through the *Fasti,* but the name is very common hereabouts; see below.

114. *Mr Hepburn:* There is no mention in the *Fasti* of a clergyman of this name in this synod, or any other, for the date 1787. If he was a clergyman he may have been of some other non-

conformist persuasion, or of the English Church.

115. *Dulsie:* Hamlet with romantic bridge on the River Findhorn, twelve miles south-east of Nairn.

116. *Findhorn River:* Rises in the Monadhliath Mountains.

117. *Cawdor:* The castle was built in 1454. Parish and village, Nairnshire. (Plate 27.)

118. *Kilravock:* Castle on the River Nairn, seven miles southwest of Nairn. Castle visited by Mary Queen of Scots in 1562, and by Charles Edward Stuart a few days before Culloden. (Plate 20.)

119. *Mrs Hugh Rose* (formerly Elizabeth Clephane): Mother of Mrs Elizabeth Rose and sister of Major James Clephane.

120. *Mrs Elizabeth Rose of Kilravock* (1747–1815): Widow of Dr Hugh Rose of Brea. Burns carried a letter of introduction to her from her cousin Henry Mackenzie. She was universally acclaimed a woman of wit, culture and musical talent. Writing to her from Edinburgh, 17 February 1788, Burns thanked her and added: 'There was something in my reception at Kilravock so different from the cold, obsequious dancing-school bow of politeness that it almost got into my head that friendship had occupied her ground without the intermediate march of acquaintance.'

121. *Fort George:* Fort on the Moray Firth, eleven miles northeast of Inverness. (Plate 31.)

122. *Inverness:* One hundred and eight miles west-north-west of Aberdeen. Royal burgh, market town and seaport. Burns stayed at the Ettles Hotel, from where he paid his compliments by letter to William Inglis. Contrary to what some modern popular historians aver, Inverness was never Jacobite in persuasion. (Plate 32.)

123. *Loch Ness:* North-east reach of the Great Glen, Invernessshire. Twenty-three miles in length.

124. *General's Hut:* That is, the hut in which General Wade (1727) lived when engineering the road along Loch Ness. Replaced by the Foyers Hotel.

125. *Falls of Foyers:* Near the mouth of the River Foyers, Inverness-shire. Burns wrote this poem on the falls:

> *Among the heathy hills and ragged woods*
> *The roaring Fyers pours his mossy floods;*
> *Till full he dashes on the rocky mounds,*
> *Where, thro' a shapeless breach, his stream resounds.*
> *As high in air the bursting torrents flow,*
> *As deep recoiling surges foam below,*
> *Prone down the rock the whitening sheet descends,*
> *And viewless Echo's ear, astonish'd, rends.*
> *Dim-seen, through rising mists and ceaseless showers,*
> *The hoary cavern, wide-surrounding, lowers.*

Still thro' the gap the struggling river toils,
And still, below, the horrid caldron boils——

In Burns's day these falls were a noble cascade of about 200 ft. (Plate 33.) In 1894–95 the spectacular character of the falls was much abated by the use of their water-power in connection with aluminium work which led to the establishment of the smart, well-sited villages of Foyers and Glenlia.

126. *Urquhart Castle:* Lies on the west side of Loch Ness, thirteen miles south-west of Inverness. Ruined in Burns's time, having been blown up at the beginning of the eighteenth century. (Plate 34.)

127. *Bailie William Inglis* (1747–1801): Provost of Inverness, 1797. A note from Burns to Inglis is extant dated 4 September 1787; it asks for a postponement of an appointment, because Burns was 'jaded to death with the fatigue of today's journey'.

128. *Culloden Moor:* On the border of Nairnshire and Inverness-shire. Site of the defeat on 16 April 1746 of the Jacobite army of Charles Edward Stuart by the Duke of Cumberland. Surprisingly little reaction here from Burns, who had strong Jacobite leanings. (Plate 35.)

129. *Kilravock:* See note 118.

130. *Alexander Grant of Cawdor* (1743–1828): Admitted as cleric 1780. Married Grace Fraser 1782. Although Burns visited Innerleithen on Monday, 14 May 1787, and stayed at the inn there, in his *Journal* of the Border Tour he makes no mention of a Mr Scott from here. But see the notes in *Robert Burns's Tour of the Borders* for references of the Scotts he did meet.

131. *Kildrummie:* A farmstead in Nairnshire, home of Lady Brae, mother-in-law of Elizabeth Rose. The house contained a very extensive library which Burns explored.

132. Burns's misspelling, actually *Miss Rose*; Mrs Elizabeth Rose's sister-in-law.

133. *Sophie Brodie:* Daughter of the naturalist and botanist James Brodie (1744–1824). His wife, the mother of Sophie, had been burnt to death in an accident at Brodie Castle in 1786. According to George Bain, Sophie married Dunbar Brodie of Burgie.

134. *Nairn:* Royal and municipal burgh and seaport, fifteen and a half miles east-north-east of Inverness. *N.B.* Henry Mackenzie provost 1785–88. See notes 16 and 111.

135. *Dr Alexander Stewart:* Son of the Jacobite John Stewart (b. 1700) of Bonskeid. Dr Stewart practised in Holland and later in Dunkeld.

136. *Hugh Falconer of Hawkerton and Lethen:* Merchant. The

Roses and the Falconers were kinsmen by marriage. Member of the Nairn Town Council.

137. *Findhorn:* A fishing village five miles north of *Forres*, a famous royal burgh and market town, twelve and a half miles west of Elgin.

138. *Elgin:* Royal burgh and county town of Morayshire, on the River Lossie. Cathedral founded in 1224. An account contemporary with Burns's visit describes Elgin as follows: 'As you approach Elgin the landscape is painted higher, the river Lossie winds between woody banks and well-cultured plains; the distant hills are generally covered with plantations of firs; and the Cathedral of Elgin . . . gives a blended assemblage of objects.' (Plate 37.)

139. *William Dunbar* (d. 1807): Writer to the Signet and Inspector-General of Stamp Duties for Scotland. Dunbar had met Burns at the Crochallan Fencibles Club and at the Canongate Kilwinning Masonic Lodge, both at Edinburgh.

140. *Spey:* See note 102. *Fochabers,* seven miles east-south-east of Elgin.

141. *Gordon Castle:* Seat of the Duke of Gordon, part dates from 1449–1684, on the border of Banff and Moray. (Plate 38.) Burns celebrated the castle in song:

> *Streams that glide in orient plains,*
> *Never bound by Winter's chains;*
> *Glowing here on golden sands,*
> *There immixed with foulest stains*
> *From Tyranny's empurpled hands:*
> *These, their richly gleaming waves,*
> *I leave the tyrants and their slaves,*
> *Give me the stream that sweetly laves*
>   *The banks by CASTLE GORDON.——*

> *Torrid forests, every gay,*
> *Shading from the burning ray*
> *Hapless wretches sold to toil;*
> *Or the ruthless Native's way,*
> *Bent on slaughter, blood and spoil:*
> *Woods that ever verdant wave,*
> *I leave the tyrant and the slave,*
> *Give me the groves that lofty brave*
>   *The storms, by CASTLE GORDON.——*

> *Wildly here without control,*
> *Nature reigns and rules the whole;*

> *In that sober, pensive mood,*
> *Dearest to the feeling soul,*
> *She plants the forest, pours the flood:*
> *Life's poor day I'll musing rave,*
> *And find at night a sheltering cave,*
> *Where waters flow and wild woods wave*
>   *By bonny CASTLE GORDON.*——

Personalities: Alexander, fourth Duke of Gordon (1743–1827), and his wife Jane Maxwell (1748–1812). Lady Charlotte (1768–1842) became Duchess of Richmond and Lennox. Lady Madelina (1772–1849) married twice: (1) Sir Robert Sinclair of Muckle, (2) Charles Fysche Palmer of Luckley Park. The Duke's other children, not mentioned by Burns: George (b. 1770), Alexander (1785–1808), Susan (1774–1828), Louisa (1776–1850), and Georgina (1781–1853) —like Burns, the Duke had several illegitimate children. It is likely that Burns met William Marshall (1748–1833), the Duke's butler, at Gordon Castle. Marshall was a keen collector of folk tunes, some of which Burns used in his manuscripts. It is likely too that Burns met the Castle Gordon medical attendant, Dr Robert Coupar. The poem 'The Young Highland Rover' is considered a consequence of this visit with its references to Castle Gordon and 'fair Strathspey'.

142. *Col. Ralph Abercrombie* (1738–1801): Later knighted, saw service in Egypt.

143. The identity of this person and 'Mr Dunbar's friend' are a matter of conjecture: they could be Charles Hay, or Adam Gillies, or Alex Gordon, all Crochallan Fencibles.

144. *James Hoy* (1747–1828): Librarian to the Duke of Gordon. Burns wrote several letters to Hoy on literary matters.

145. *Cullen:* Five and a half miles west-north-west of Portsoy, Banffshire.

Principal J. C. Shairp remarks in *Robert Burns* (Macmillan, 1879), p. 70: 'An intelligent boy, who was guide to Burns and Nicol from Cullen to Duff House, gave long afterwards his remembrances of that day. Among these this occurs. The boy was asked by Nicol if he had read Burns's poems, and which of them he liked best. The boy replied, "I was much entertained with *The Twa Dogs* and *Death and Dr Hornbrook*, but I like best *The Cotter's Saturday Night*, although it made me *greet* when my father had me to read it to my mother". Burns, with a sudden start, looked at the boy intently and patting his shoulder said, "Well, my callant, I don't wonder at your *greeting* at reading the poem; it made me greet more than once when I was writing it at my father's fireside" ...'

In *A Burns's Companion* (Aberdeen: Blair, 1957), W. B. Campbell states that Burns is thought to have visited the farm of Thornybank (built 1759), three miles south of Buckie. Here came the inspiration for the poem 'A' the lads o' Thornie-bank'. The 'Lady Onlie, honest lucky' therein mentioned is not now identifiable as a local.

146. *Banff:* Capital of the county at the north of the Devon river, fifty miles north-west of Aberdeen. The town received its first charter from Malcolm IV in 1163. Nicol and Burns breakfasted with Dr George Chapman, headmaster of Banff Grammar School. Nicol had been a junior master at Dumfries Academy under Chapman. For conversations see *Chambers Edinburgh Journal* (viii, p. 405).

147. *Portsoy Bay:* In the parish of Fordyce, N. Banffshire, the town lies eight and a half miles west of Banff. The tradition that Burns also visited Sandend, two miles away, is today uncorroborated by documentary evidence.

148. *Duff House:* Occupied by James, second Earl of Fife, when Burns visited; later the house was presented to the citizens of Banff. According to George Imlach (1775–1863), Burns examined the library and oil paintings at Duff House. Imlach was the son of the Banff agent for the Aberdeen bank, and was dux of the Banff Grammar School. He acted as guide to the poet and Nicol (cf. note 145). (Plate 40.)

149. *Newbyth:* Village in N. Aberdeenshire.

150. *Buchan:* District extending some forty miles from Ythan to the Deveron in north-east Aberdeenshire: chief towns, Peterhead and Fraserburgh. *Old Deer:* Parish and village in Aberdeenshire. Contains ruin of a Cistercian abbey of the thirteenth century.

151. *Peterhead:* Parish, burgh and seaport of north-east Aberdeenshire, thirty-three miles north-east of Aberdeen: centre of herring fishing. (Plate 41.) Local records, both in public possession and the Burns Club, make no mention of Burns's visit.

152. *Bullers of Buchan:* Huge rocky cauldron, six miles south of Peterhead. *Slains Castle:* Burns's misspelling; castle demolished in 1594 by James VI.

153. *Ellon:* Parish nineteen miles north-east of Aberdeen. 'Lord Aberdeen' is George Gordon, third Earl of Aberdeen (1722–1801).

154. *Aberdeen:* County town of Aberdeenshire, royal burgh, charter granted in 1179 by William the Lyon. The town lies between the Dee and the Don rivers. Prominent University. Burns stayed at the New Inn, Castle Street. The local paper of the time

makes only passing reference to Burns's visit. Statue of Burns by Henry Bain Smith, unveiled 15 September 1892.

155. *James Chalmers* (1742–1810): Editor of the *Aberdeen Journal*.

156. *John Ross:* Professor of Hebrew at King's College, 1767–90. *Alexander Fraser Tytler* (1747–1813): Joint-Professor of Universal History at Edinburgh University.

157. *Mr Marshall:* For some considerable time now there has been much controversy among Burns scholars as to who this person was. Several editors have identified this person as John Marshall, who was noted as a prominent Aberdeen poet by William Walker in his *Bards of Bon-Accord*. While a student this John Marshall was one of the writers for the *Aberdeen Censor*: As the first number of the *Censor* was published in 1825, it is obvious that this Marshall was too young to have met Burns in 1787. In his edition of *The Life and Works of Robert Burns* (Edinburgh, 1828), Robert Chambers notes, 'Marshall may have been William Marshall (1748–1833), factor to the Duke of Gordon, author of Scottish Airs, Melodies, etc., for piano, violin and violincello'. However, J. M. Bulloch in his biography of William Marshall says: 'It is doubtful . . . whether Burns ever met the composer'. Burns, of course, also knew William Marshall (1745–1818), the experimental agriculturalist who wrote *Rural Economy of England*: Burns certainly read part of this work (see letter to Robert Graham of Fintry, 13 May 1789). A search through Burns's letters has not, furthermore, made this identity of 'Mr Marshall' any clearer.

158. *Andrew Shirrefs* (1762–1807)*:* Poet and crippled son of a builder in Aberdeen's Gallowgate. Famous for *Poems, chiefly in the Scottish Dialect* (1790), in imitation of Burns.

159. *Rev. John Skinner* (1744–1816)*:* Primus of the Scottish Episcopal Church, son of Rev. John Skinner (1721–1807), author of the song 'Tullochgorum', which Burns described as 'the best Scotch Song ever Scotland saw'.

160. *Professor Thomas Gordon* (c. 1714–97)*:* In succession Professor of Humanity and Philosophy in King's College, Aberdeen.

161. *Stonehaven:* Seaport and county town of Kincardineshire, sixteen miles south-east of Aberdeen. Important fishing centre.

162. See Appendix I for notes on Burns's Kincardine relatives. The Robert Burns herein mentioned was the elder brother of John Burnes, the author of 'Thrummy Cap'.

163. *Laurencekirk:* A small market town in south Kincardineshire. (The identity of the lady herein noted has not been traced.) In 1972 a plaque was set up on the Gardenstone Arms Hotel to commemorate the poet's stay.

164. *Howe of the Mearns:* Colloquial name for that quarter of Kincardine.

165. *Craigo:* Village in Angus, five miles north-west of Montrose.

166. *Auchmithie:* Quoad sacra parish and fishing village of Angus, three and a half miles north-east of Arbroath. (Plate 39.)

167. *Ye Geary Pot*, or 'Gaylet Pot': A rocky cavern along the Angus coastline.

168. *Arbroath:* Formerly Aberbrothock, seventeen miles north-east of Dundee. Abbey founded by William the Lyon in 1178. The Fairport of Sir Walter Scott's *The Antiquary* (1816). (Plate 42.)

169. *Dundee:* City, a royal parliamentary and municipal burgh in the county of Angus. Extensive dockyards and university complexes. The steeple to which Burns refers is the fifteenth-century tower of the City Churches, also known as St Mary's Tower. Replica of the statue of Burns in New York, by Sir John Steel, unveiled 16 October 1880. (Plate 44.)

170. *Tayfrith:* This is merely Firth of Tay.

171. *Broughty Castle:* This fifteenth-century castle was a ruin in Burns's day; it was restored 1860–61.

172. Margaret (b. 1743), Jean (b. 1747), and Janet (b. 1753), daughters of the Rev. David Scott of Auchterhouse.

173. *Rev. Andrew Mitchell* (1729–94): Minister of Aberlemno, Forfar, 1750–94. He was a brother-in-law to the Rev. David Scott mentioned in note 172.

174. *Rev. John Bruce* (1758–1817): Minister of Forfar, 1782–1817.

175. *Mr Anderson:* Husband of Jean Scott; see note 172.

176. *Mrs Greenfield:* Wife of the Rev. William Greenfield (d. 1827), Professor of Rhetoric and Minister of St Andrew's Church, Edinburgh, and later of the High Church.

The reference to 'Bess Scott' is curious. The Rev. D. Scott had only one daughter called Elizabeth, who died in 1751. It may have been a family nickname for one of the other sisters.

177. *Carse of Gowrie:* A fertile tract of land in the counties of Perth and Angus, along the north bank of the Tay, fifteen miles long.

178. *Perth:* Once called St John's Town, this royal and ancient city lies twenty-two miles south-west of Dundee. The oldest building Burns would see was the cruciform church of St John. Here John Knox preached his famous Reformation sermon. In Burns's day there would still be plenty of people around who spoke Gaelic. 'The Fair City' remained fiercely Jacobite.

179. *Huntly:* In the parish of Longforgan, seven miles west of Dundee.

180. *Sir Stewart Thriepland of Fingask* (1716–1805)*:* A fervent Jacobite, and President of the Royal College of Physicians of Edinburgh (1766).

181. *Scone:* Parish and village in Perthshire, two miles north-east of Perth. Burns visited the palace which occupies the site of an abbey founded in 1411. A former capital of Scotland, Scone was long the place where the Scottish kings were crowned.

182. *Taybridge:* The stone bridge built in 1766.

183. *Mr & Mrs Hastings:* Members of the family of Hastings of Perth, who were mostly merchants.

184. *Major Scot:* Brother of David Scott of that Perth family.

185. *Castle Gowrie:* Perthshire, scene of the mysterious plot against James VI and I. (Plate 46.)

186. *Endermay:* Note modern spelling of Invermay, seat, Perthshire.

187. A song founded on the sad story of Bessie Bell and Mary Gray: 'In 1645, when the plague struck Perth, these two maidens betook themselves to a riverside bower to avoid catching it, by living in isolation. Unfortunately they were visited by a young man from the plague-stricken town, admirer of one, or both, and as a consequence caught the infection from him after all, and died.' The two girls were buried together at Dronach Haugh, on the banks of the River Almond; as the old ballad relates:

> *They thought to lie in Methven Kirk*
> *Amang their noble kin*
> *But they maun[a] lie on Lyn(e)doch brae[b]*
> *To beek fornent[c] the sun.*
> *O Bessie Bell and Mary Gray*
> *They were twa bonnie lassies*
> *They biggit[d] a bower on yon burn-brae[e]*
> *And theekit it o'er wi' rashes[f].*

[a] must; [b] river-bank; [c] bathe/facing; [d] built; [e] that stream; [f] thatched it over with rushes.

The verse is not attributed to Burns. Today this grave is on private land (on the Mansfield Estate near the hamlet of Pitcairngreen), and the spot was railed at a later date than the burial by one of the Lord Lynedochs, who set up the epitaph: *They lived—they loved—they died*, in allusion to this old tale that the girls were in love with the same man. How curious that this theme did not appeal to Burns and set him rhyming !

188. *Mrs Alexander Belsches:* Of Invermay. Their mansion in Burns's time was in the valley of the Earn.

189. *Miss Stirling:* Younger daughter of the Stirlings of Keir.

190. *Kinross:* On the west side of Loch Leven, thirteen and three-quarter miles north by east of Dunfermline. In the loch was the island on which Mary Queen of Scots was imprisoned. While in this area Burns picked up the words and pipe tune of 'Hey ca' thro' ' which he reworked in 1792. The original is a traditional Fife song:

> *Up wi' the carls of Dysart,*
>   *And the lads o' Buckhiven,*
> *And the Kimmers o' Largo,*
>   *And the lasses o' Leven.*
>   *Hey ca' thro' ca' thro'*
>   *For we hae mickle a do,*
>   *Hey ca' thro' ca' thro'*
>   *For we hae mickle a do.*

> *We hae tales to tell,*
>   *And we hae sangs to sing;*
> *We hae pennies to spend,*
>   *And we hae pints to bring.*
>   *Hey ca' thro' &c.*

> *We'll live a' our days,*
>   *And them that come behin'*
> *Let them do the like,*
>   *And spend the gear they win.*
>   *Hey ca' thro' &c.*

191. *Queensferry:* Small village on the north shore of the Firth of Forth, two miles south of Inverkeithing.

Tour of Stirlingshire with Dr Adair

On returning to Edinburgh from his tour with Nicol, Burns turned once more to the business of earning a living. He toyed for a while with the two opportunities which had presented themselves to him; the development of his farming interests, or to join the Excise as an officer. His mind too was occupied with the task of getting William Creech his publisher to settle his business.

After a further two weeks of waiting at Edinburgh Burns set out on another round of visits. For his fourth tour of his native land, Burns chose Dr James McKittrick Adair (1765–1802) as his companion. The son of an Ayr doctor and a kinsman of Mrs Frances Anna Dunlop (1730–1815), James Adair had studied in Geneva and subsequently at Edinburgh University, where he graduated in medicine: Adair practised in the Pleasance, Edinburgh, then moved to Harrogate in Yorkshire, where he died. Burns had been introduced to Adair, of course, by the Rev. Dr George Lawrie (1727–99), minister of Loudoun. Burns did not keep a journal of this jaunt, but Adair later supplied Dr Currie with an account (1798).

Adair's Account of the Stirlingshire Tour

[*Leaving Edinburgh about 4 October 1787*] We rode by Linlithgow and Carron[192] to Stirling. We visited the iron-works at Carron, with which the poet was forcibly struck. The resemblance between that place and its inhabitants to the cave of the Cyclops,[193] which must have occurred to every classical reader, presented itself to Burns. At Stirling the

E [51]

prospects from the Castle strongly interested him; his national feelings had, in a former visit, been powerfully excited by the ruinous and roofless state of the hall in which the Scottish Parliaments had frequently been held. His indignation had vented itself in some imprudent, but not unpoetical lines, which had given much offence, and which he took this opportunity of erasing, by breaking the pane of the window at the inn on which they were written.[194]

At Stirling we met with a company of travellers from Edinburgh, among whom was a character in many respects congenial with that of Burns. This was Nicol, one of the teachers of the High Grammar-School at Edinburgh—the same wit and power of conversation; the same fondness for convivial society, and thoughtlessness of to-morrow, characterised them both; Jacobitical principles in politics were common to both of them; and these have been suspected, since the revolution in France, to have given place in each to opinions apparently opposite. I regret that I have preserved no *memorabilia* of their conversation, either on this or other occasions, when I happened to meet them together. Many songs were sung; which I mention for the sake of observing, that then when Burns was called on in his turn, he was accustomed, instead of singing, to recite one or other of his own shorter poems, with a tone and emphasis, which though not correct or harmonious, were impressive and pathetic. This he did on the present occasion.

From Stirling we went next morning through the romantic and fertile vale of Devon to Harvieston, in Clackmannanshire, then inhabited by Mrs Hamilton,[195] with the younger part of whose family Burns had been previously acquainted. He introduced me to the family, and then was formed my first acquaintance with Mrs Hamilton's eldest daughter to whom I have been married for nine years.[196] Thus was I indebted to Burns for a connexion from which I have derived, and expect further to derive, much happiness.

During a residence of about ten days at Harvieston, we made excursions to various parts of the surrounding scenery, inferior to none in Scotland in beauty, sublimity, and romantic interest; particularly Castle Campbell, the ancient seat of the family of Argyll;[197] and the famous cataract of the Devon, called the Caldron-linn;[198] and the Rumbling Bridge, a single broad arch, thrown by the devil, if tradition is to be believed, accross [*sic*] the river, at the height of about one hundred feet above its bed.

A visit to Mrs Bruce of Clackmannan,[199] a lady above ninety, the lineal descendant of that race which gave the Scottish throne its brightest ornament, interested his feelings powerfully. This venerable dame, with characteristic dignity informed me on my observing that I believed she was descended from the family of Robert Bruce, that Robert Bruce was sprung from her family. Though almost deprived of speech by a paralytic affection, she preserved her hospitality and urbanity. She was in possession of the hero's helmet and two-handed sword, with which she conferred on Burns and myself the honour of knighthood, remarking that she had a better right to confer that title than *some people*.[200] You will of course conclude that the old lady's political tenets were as Jacobital as the poet's, a conformity which contributed not a little to the cordiality of our reception and entertainment. She gave us her first toast after dinner, 'Awa Uncos', or Away the Strangers! Who these strangers were, you will readily understand.

At Dunfermline[201] we visited the ruined abbey, and the abbey church, now consecrated to Presbyterian worship. Here I mounted the cutty stool, or stool of repentance,[202] assuming the character of a penitent for fornication; while Burns from the pulpit addressed to me a ludicrous reproof and exhortation, parodied from that which had been delivered to himself in Ayrshire,[203] where he had, as he assured me, once been one of the seven who mounted the *seat of shame* together.

In the church, two broad flag-stones marked the grave of Robert Bruce for whose memory Burns had more than common veneration. He knelt and kissed with sacred fervour, and heartily (*suus ut mos erat*) execrated the worse than Gothic neglect of the first of Scottish heroes.

While Adair dallied with his future wife Charlotte Hamilton at Harvieston, Burns made two small excursions on his own account. One to John Ramsay of Ochtertyre, near Stirling, in Kincardine, and the other to Sir William Murray, at the less famous Ochtertyre in Strathearn, near Crieff.

John Ramsay (1736–1814), the son of a wealthy lawyer, had been schooled at Dalkeith and became a noteworthy classicist at Edinburgh University. Although he never practised, he studied law in his father's advocates' office, and ultimately became a country gentleman; with the reputation of being a good landlord and an experimenter in agricultural techniques. Ramsay was a prominent 'Edinburgh figure' and Sir Walter Scott used him as a prototype for Johnathan Oldbuck in *The Antiquary.*

Burns was introduced to Ramsay through the blind minor poet Dr Thomas Blacklock (1721–91). Later Ramsay was to supply information of his conversations with Burns, to Currie. Ramsay considered Burns's principles 'abundantly motley, he being a Jacobite, and Arminian and a Socinian'. Ramsay went on:

> I have been in the company of many men of genius, some of them poets, but never witnessed such flashes of intellectual brightness as from him, the impulse of the moment, sparks of celestial fire! I never was more delighted, therefore, than with his company for two days, *tête-à-tête*. In a mixed company I should have made little of him, for in the gamester's phrase, he did not always know when to play off and when to play on . . . I not only proposed to him the writing of a play similar to *The Gentle Shepherd, qualem decet esse sororem*, but Scottish Georgics, a subject which Thomson has by no means exhausted in his *Seasons*. What beautiful a landscape of rural life and manner might not have been expected from

a pencil so faithful and so forcible as his, which could have exhibited scenes as familiar and interesting as those in *The Gentle Shepherd* which everyone who knows our swains in their unadulterated state instantly recognises as true to nature ! But to have executed either of these plans, steadiness and abstraction from company were wanting, not talents !

Sir William Murray (d. 1800) was a cousin of Robert Graham of Fintry (see pp. 20 and 39), to whom it will be remembered Burns, in the letter of 13 May 1789, referred to Sir William as an 'honoured friend'. Sir William and Lady Augusta Murray were the parents of Sir George Murray (1772–1846), Wellington's quarter-master general in the Peninsula: both he and his brother, the later Sir Patrick Murray (b. 1770), met Burns on this occasion. While at Ochtertyre, Burns met 'the flower of Strathmore', Euphemia Murray of Lintrose (b. 1769), for whom he wrote 'Song.—Composed at Auchtertyre on Miss Euphemia Murray of Lentrose', which was set to the tune 'Andrew an' his cutty gun'. According to tradition, Euphemia Murray was not impressed by Burns's honour.

Burns's other 'Ochtertyre piece' was the poem 'On scaring some Water-Fowl in Loch-Turit, a wild scene among the Hills of Oughtertyre': About this poem there is this note to be found in the *Glenriddel Ms*: 'This was the production of a solitary afternoon's walk from Oughtertyre House.—I lived there, Sir William's guest, for two or three weeks, and was much flattered by my hospitable reception.—What a pity that the mere emotions of gratitude are so impotent in this world ! 'Tis lucky that, as we are told, they will be of some avail in the world to come——'

It is interesting to note that in his narrative Adair gives the length of their stay at Harvieston as 'about ten days'. Burns, however, in a letter to William Cruickshank (d. 1795) wrote: 'I was storm-steaded two days at the foot of the Ochel Hills, with Mr Tait of Harvieston and Mr Johnson of Alva'. Piecing together local information concerning the poet's visit to Alva, William Harvey noted the following:

It appears that during the time he was in the Hillfoots
district he journeyed to Alva and remained over night.
He visited Mr Johnson, the first laird of Alva of that
name, who was then the inhabitant of Alva House, and
who, in earlier years, had fought at Plassey. It might be
inferred from Burns's letter that he was the guest of
Mr Johnson during his stay in Alva, but, locally, it is
believed that this is not the case. The tradition is that he
passed the night at Courthill House, which was at that
time occupied as an inn by a person of the name of Hume.
The building, which is situated in Ochil Street, is now
used as a dwellinghouse, and on the occasion of [*William
Harvey's*] visit . . . found that the inhabitants were
quite familiar with the story of the poet's stay, although
they made no endeavour to impose credulity by pointing
out the room or shewing the bed in which he had slept.

William Harvey also mentions that while Burns was in Alva
he renewed acquaintance with Elizabeth 'Lucky' Black (1754–
1823), whom he had originally met at Mauchline. At the time
Elizabeth Black kept a public house in Alva and tradition has
it that Burns drank ale here with a number of local worthies,
including grand-uncle James Dawson and his crony, John
Morrison.

After their sojourn in Stirlingshire, Burns and Adair
returned to Edinburgh via Queensferry, and the tour was
concluded 20 October 1787. During the nineteenth century the
claim of one Thomas Morrison that he was the man who
ferried Burns over the Firth of Forth was widely circulated;
documentary evidence, however, has not been found to
substantiate this claim.

Notes

Tour of Stirlingshire with Dr Adair

192. See note 29, pages 31-32.

193. *Cyclops:* Different accounts are given of the Cyclops, but Homer speaks of them as one-eyed giant shepherds in Sicily, the chief being Polyphemus.

194. See note 40, page 33.

195. See note 41, page 34. Here too was Margaret Chalmers. See Appendix II.

196. *Charlotte Hamilton* (1763–1806)*:* Elder daughter of John Hamilton of Kype. She married Dr Adair, 11 November 1789.

197. *Castle Campbell:* Castle (now ruined) a mile north of Dollar in Clackmannanshire. It was acquired by the Earls of Argyll in 1493, and received the name of Castle Campbell in place of its former one, Castle Gloume.

198. See note 43, page 34.

199. *Mrs Catherine Bruce* (1696–1791)*:* Daughter of Alexander Bruce of the Newton branch of the family. She married Henry Bruce of Clackmannan and lived in the old tower (now a ruin) at the west of Clackmannan village. (Plate 50.)

200. She was referring to the Hanoverians in general and George III (1738–1820) in particular. Mrs Bruce also 'knighted' Dr Jamieson, editor of the *Scots Dictionary*, when he called on her a month later. According to Jamieson, and tradition, as the poet knelt before her he attempted to kiss her hand: 'What ails ye at ma' moo'?' she is reported to have said. The sword and helmet fell (via the seventh Earl) to the Earls of Elgin, who display them at Broomhall, the seat of the earls two and a half miles west of Dunfermline, where they are still to be seen. It should be noted, however, that the helmet is seventeenth century in origin and belonged not to Robert the Bruce, but to Colonel Henry Bruce, an ardent royalist, who was killed at Worcester (1651).

201. *Dunfermline:* A royal burgh of Fife, fifteen miles north-east of Edinburgh. The fine Norman nave, which is all the Reformers spared in their assault (1560) on this abbey, founded in 1072 by

Queen Margaret, wife of King Malcolm Ceanmore, now forms the vestibule of the New Abbey Church. Queen Margaret, King Malcolm and Robert Bruce lie buried therein. It was at Dunfermline in 1581 that James VI signed the first National Covenant, and where in 1650 Charles II signed the Dunfermline Declaration. (Plate 49.)

The sole marking ever to be placed on the grave of Robert Bruce was a 19th century brass. The tomb was only discovered in 1818 in the centre of the choir, when the building of the New Abbey was taking place. The stone which Adair fancifully says that Burns kissed may have covered the grave of some ancient Scot—*it certainly did not cover that of Robert Bruce.* (See also: 'Burns and the Kingdom of Fife', an address delivered to Dunfermline Rotary Club in 1946 by Rev. William MacMillan.)

202. See note 18, page 30.

203. Burns made his first penitential appearance 9 July 1786.

Epilogue

Burns's tours of the Highlands and Stirlingshire leave the reader with a number of enigmatic questions. Unfortunately in his own accounts of his travels Burns is perversely vague, and gives the minimum of information about the places he visited and the people he met; an unusual trait in a writer. The notes set out herein will undoubtedly answer many of the biographical questions which arise, but others persistently remain. For instance, Burns, as a spontaneous poet, found himself more at home with the rhyme and the poetic ditty than he did with the journal or the essay: Consequently his biographers must look for clues, in his contemporary and later works, to find out what he was really thinking while touring, remembering too that Burns did not have the necessary solitude, while on tour, to actually compose anything of spontaneous genius.

His tours of Stirlingshire and the Highlands gave Burns much food for thought, but at first he was presented with nagging questions concerning the ambiguity of his position. Undoubtedly he had been made welcome as something of a literary wonder at gentlemen's houses wherever he went. Furthermore he was allowed to talk freely with their pretty daughters. All the time, however, he felt he was being kept 'in his place'. Ebullient, he often forgot his station and treated these genteel young ladies as though they were knickerless country lasses. More than once, the peasant poet went too far, and the young lady, as he once expressed it himself, 'flew off in a tangent of female dignity and reserve'. As he later told Agnes MacLehose ('Clarinda'), he was frustrated at both a psychological and a physical level.

[59]

It is unlikely that Burns made any bibliographical preparation on the Highlands before he set off on his tours. He was never a man to do prior research on a jaunt, although such texts as Thomas Pennant's *A Tour of Scotland 1769* (Chester, 1771), and Samuel Johnson's *A Journey to the Western Isles of Scotland* (1775), were known to his friends among the *literati*. Burns therefore saw the Highlands with no preconceived ideas.

On his tour Burns would see that the years which followed that decisive battle at Culloden Moor had exaggerated the differences between his native Lowlands and the Highland Scotland he visited, differences which became a standing challenge to Scotland's unity and progress. Economic changes had transformed life in the English-speaking parts of Scotland, but the impact was patchy, weak and intermittent in the Highlands. Deeply attached to their native Gaelic, loyal to the clan chiefs and clinging to their traditional ways, the men of the northern regions ignored and resisted the 'English' improvements that were welcomed south of that geological fault between Dunbarton and Stonehaven. In 1787 Burns witnessed the last gleam of the true Celtic Twilight, which eventually led to the depopulation, starvation and poverty, which the statesmen, economists and churchmen were not able, or were not willing, to arrest. Even then in Burns's day, the Highlands were overpopulated in terms of resources. For while those parts with easy access to the Lowlands were able to 'export' timber, horses, cheese and butter, and the fishing villages part of their catches, the main 'cash crop' of the Highlands was the rearing of small black cattle.*

After 1746 the clan chiefs became landowners as such, with a taste for the fine life, which eventually drained the local resources. Next to the clan chief came the tacksman, a rent-paying gentleman; thence came the peasant farmers and the lowly crofters and labourers. The latter lived in rough-hewn

---

* Pryde, G. S. *Scotland from 1603 to the present day.* London: Nelson, 1962.

'black houses', without either glass or slates, with animals living a communal life with the inhabitants. Carts were almost unknown, and horses only for the fortunate for transport and ploughing. Sheep were raised in small numbers for their wool and mutton, and even then this meat was mainly eaten by substantial tenants. Beef too was scarce and oatmeal was the basis of traditional diets, with some barley-bread, herrings and milk. Clothing consisted mainly of woollens, home spun, home woven and home dyed, with rawhide brogues.

All through Burns's day there was no movement between the classes and no hope of the peasant bettering his lot: Burns saw that the Highland society was held together by common beliefs and mutual loyalties and bigotry, and by the bond of fear and suffering. This was the background of Burns's comment: 'Where savage streams tumble over savage mountains, thinly overspread with savage flocks, which starvingly support as savage inhabitants.'

A constant theme in Samuel Johnson's *Journey* touches on contrasts between England and Scotland: Burns concerned himself mainly with Scotland's poor and Scotland's rich. Yet his schizoid mentality made him at once a hater of poverty and those who caused it, and a devotee of the activities and extravagances of the gentry. Johnson praises the smoothness of the Scottish roads and lanes, and the fine buildings of New Aberdeen, explicitly comparing the case in England: but Burns's interest lay not in fishing villages, carses and architecture, but in humanity.

Burns had begun his career as a singer of local songs, but now as he travelled around his ambition became clear to him: he was to be a poet of Scotland! On his tours, then, he absorbed local traditions, cocked an ear to local ditties and songs and other fragments half forgotten. Shortly after his tours Burns was to begin his great opus of re-creating single-handed an almost entire embodiment of Scottish folksong. Thanks to his attentive folkloric interest on his tours, he was able to anchor song after song to the particular landscape and topography, giving 'a local habitation and a name' to many of his productions. Nevertheless, Burns did not have a strictly 'romantic' approach to Nature, which he always regarded with a farmer's eye. Although it may be said that what ties Burns had with the older poetic tradition of Scotland, his nature poems were the closest link. His landscapes were peopled with bonnie lasses and calloused hinds seeking pleasure after a day's 'moil and toil'. Even the Falls of Foyers, for instance, led only to trite generalities. And yet he was not bereft of historical emotion. He greatly liked visiting ruins and historic scenes and saw with grief and pride the fields of Culloden and Bannockburn. Charles Edward Stuart (died 31 January 1788), of course, was still alive when Burns visited Culloden, although the Duke of Cumberland had been dead for over twenty years. Thus Burns still had the benefit of the *débâcle* being within living memory; so that many of the people he met hereabouts would be able to supply fresh contemporary comment. But Burns, as a patriot, was curiously silent in prose concerning 'the scenes of grief'.

In 1787 it was still unfashionable to be a Jacobite; and Burns was bloodyminded enough to be forthright and declare his views. But he seems to have buried his grief within himself. Or was it that his 'republicanism' was welling up to disconcert his patriotic feelings? We shall never know, for such was the juxtaposition of Burns's Pittitism and Jacobism. It is interesting to note that Whiggery as late as the early years of the nineteenth century was still used as a term of abuse. *Vide* the comment by Mrs Grant of Laggan: 'Whig was an appellation of comprehensive reproach. It was used to designate a character made up of negatives; one who had neither ear for music, nor taste for poetry, no pride of ancestry; no heart for attachment; no soul for honour . . . A Whig, in short, was what all Highlanders cordially hated—a cold, selfish, formal character.' Burns therefore had to watch his tongue.

Even so these emotions of politics, history and traditionalism were fleeting for Burns when compared with his concern for environmental problems and the scraping of a living from the cruel land. They lasted long enough though for him to be rudimentarily inspired, although he overstates the case himself. 'My journey through the Highlands was perfectly inspiring', he wrote to Patrick Miller of Dalswinton, 'and I hope I have laid in a good stock of new poetical ideas from it.' His 'Robert Bruce's Address to his army at Bannockburn' and 'Scots wha hae' stand testimony to that; and to a lesser extent 'Macpherson's Farewell', which we can trace back to the Duff House interlude.

Yet, in truth, Burns *used* very little of his acquired experiences of his native land for original works. Was he depressed? Was he disenchanted? Was his idealistic attitude to the place Caledonia played in the world demoralised when he saw for himself what war, bad farming, clearances and so on had done? Indeed, Burns's reactions to battles and heroism were overplayed and made into platitudinous tushery in the 1880s and 1890s. What comes from his Highland tour is the feeling of depression of the soul. Undoubtedly Burns went through mental stress on his tours: and this was made no easier by his forced cultivation of the upper-class cult for the picturesque. Instead of pure Burns, the tours gave him Burns *à la* Addison, Dyer, Byron and Thomson: indifferent verses shot through with the thoughts of others.* Yet through it all there is a glimmer of Burns's genius. His Highland tours were neither the making nor the breaking of him as a man or as a poet; but they did show him how difficult to live with were his Muse and his Conscience.

---

* Ritter, O. *Quellenstudien zu Robert Burns 1773–1791*. Berlin, 1901.

Appendix I

Robert Burns's Kincardineshire relatives

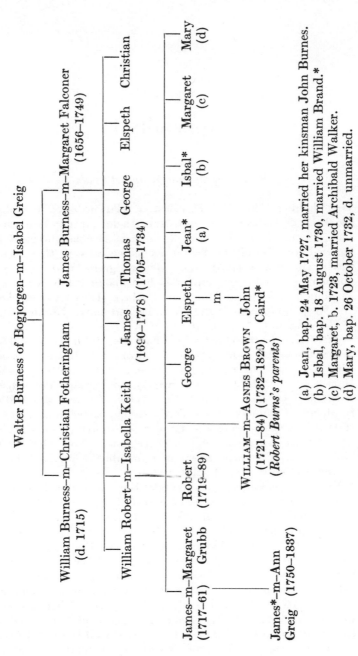

Walter Burness of Bogjorgen–m–Isabel Greig

William Burness–m–Christian Fotheringham (d. 1715)

James Burness–m–Margaret Falconer (1656–1749)

William Robert–m–Isabella Keith

James (1620–1778)

Thomas (1705–1734)

George

Elspeth

Christian

George

Elspeth
m
John Caird*

WILLIAM–m–AGNES BROWN (1721–84) (1732–1820) (*Robert Burns's parents*)

James–m–Margaret Grubb (1717–61)

Robert (1719–89)

Jean* (a)

Isbal* (b)

Margaret (c)

Mary (d)

James*–m–Ann Greig (1750–1837)

(a) Jean, bap. 24 May 1727, married her kinsman John Burnes.
(b) Isbal, bap. 18 August 1730, married William Brand.*
(c) Margaret, b. 1723, married Archibald Walker.
(d) Mary, bap. 26 October 1732, d. unmarried.

* These are the relatives Burns mentions meeting during his tour with William Nicol.

Appendix II

Robert Burns and Margaret Chalmers

The Chalmers–Hamilton–Harvieston relationship is complicated for Burns devotees to work out. Nevertheless, it may be considered thus. Thomas Murdoch of Cumloden had three daughters: Barbara married John Hamilton of Kype as his second wife, thus becoming Gavin Hamilton's (1751–1805, Burns's great friend and correspondent) step-mother; Euphemia had married John Chalmers of Fingland and had two daughters, Cochran (later Lady Mackenzie) and Margaret ('Peggy'); and Charlotte had married John Tait, WS, of Harvieston, Clackmannan.

After the death of his wife Charlotte, John Tait invited his sister-in-law, the widow Barbara Hamilton, to live at Harvieston with her son and daughters Grace and Charlotte (i.e. Gavin Hamilton's half-brother and sisters), to manage his household until his own daughter grew up. When she too was widowed, Euphemia Chalmers, John Tait's second sister-in-law, came to Harvieston. Thus were the families in residence at Harvieston when Burns visited on Monday, 27 August 1787 and October 1787: but Margaret Chalmers, it will be remembered, was at Edinburgh on the poet's first visit to Harvieston.

Margaret Chalmers was born about the year 1763; the exact date is not known. Her father, John, and all her paternal forbears had associations with estate farming, and Margaret was born at her father's property at Fingland, Kirkcudbrightshire. According to various of the poet's biographers, she was that type of woman whom Burns was bound to meet sooner or later on his tours: the balanced, sensible Scots female, who could be lively and amusing, yet of the 'no nonsense' variety. Burns was undoubtedly interested in Margaret Chalmers sexually, but because of her nature, she would have put him firmly back in his place should he have stepped too far. Burns was, of course, never on sexual terms with women of a better class than himself, or with any woman who was in any degree his mental equal.* Others have described Margaret Chalmers variously as quiet, intelligent, accomplished, vivacious, abounding in commonsense, friendly, charming, and a woman of literary tastes.

Although Burns himself says that he first met Margaret Chalmers in the Ochils, he was often vague in his biographical statements, and it is likely that he originally made her acquaintance when her father lived at Mauchline. Certainly it was not for the first time that Burns had come across her when she sang and played at the house of blind Dr Thomas Blacklock (1721–91) at Edinburgh.

Margaret Chalmers was a small girl, compact and svelte. A relative, describing her to Robert Chambers, said: 'In early life, when her hazel eyes were large and bright and her teeth white and regular, her face possessed a charm not always the result of the accompaniment of fine features. She was short, but her figure was faultless. Her conversation was cheerful, but intelligent. She talked rarely of books, yet greatly liked reading. She spoke readily and well, but preferred listening to others.'

In a sisterly way Margaret Chalmers was good for Burns, and it is clear that he felt at ease in her company. Whether *tête à tête*, or on paper, he was relaxed: for his letters to her are amongst his best and she exercised a refining influence upon the poet that only Agnes Maclehose was to outmatch.†

That Burns was in love with Margaret Chalmers is quite evident from his writings. In that letter, which, though undated, J. de Lancey Fergusson places in January 1787, Burns addressed Margaret Chalmers as 'My Dear Countrywoman' and expresses obvious love: 'I know you will laugh at it, when I tell you that your Pianoforte and you together have play'd the deuce somehow, about my heart. I was once a zealous Devotee to your Sex, but you know the black story at home. My breast has been widowed these many months, and I thought myself proof against the fascinating witchcraft; but I am afraid you will "feelingly convince me what I am". I say, I am afraid, because I am not sure what is the matter with me, I have one miserable bad symptom which I

---

* Some critics have suggested that Agnes Maclehose ('Clarinda', qv) was an exception, but they can never prove it documentarily.
† According to Robert Hartley Cromek, Charlotte Hamilton Adair destroyed Margaret's letters to Burns. But this seems odd, for some letters have survived. If Cromek's story is correct, why the obviously selective destruction? It is interesting to note that although Burns did not often date his drafts of letters the Margaret Chalmers missives surviving have been dated.

F

doubt threatens ill: when you whisper, or look kindly to another, it gives me a draught of damnation.'

During November 1787 Burns addressed two love songs to Margaret Chalmers:

Where braving angry Winter's storms, to the tune 'Neil Gow's Lamentation for Abercairney'; it appeared in the *Scots Musical Museum* in 1788:

> *Where braving angry Winter's storms*
> *The lofty Ochels rise,*
> *Far in their shade, my Peggy's charms*
> *First blest my wondering eyes.—*
>
> *As one who by some savage stream*
> *A lonely gem surveys*
> *Astonish'd doubly marks it beam*
> *With art's most polish'd blaze.—*
>
> *Blest be the wild, sequester'd glade*
> *And blest the day and hour,*
> *Where Peggy's charms I first survey'd,*
> *When first I felt their pow'r.—*
>
> *The tyrant Death with grim controul*
> *May seize my fleeting breath,*
> *But tearing Peggy from my soul*
> *Must be a stronger death.—*

Secondly, *My Peggy's face*, which first appeared in George Thomson's *Selected Scottish Airs*—to an unauthorised air in 1801. Burns originally intended it for the air *Ha a chaillich air no Dheith*.

> *My Peggy's face, my Peggy's form,*
> *The frost of hermit age might warm;*
> *My Peggy's worth, my Peggy's mind,*
> *Might charm the first of human kind.*
>
> *I love my Peggy's angel air,*
> *Her face so truly heav'nly fair,*
> *Her native grace so void of art,*
> *But I adore my Peggy's heart.*
>
> *The lily's hue, the rose's die,*
> *The kindling lustre of an eye;*
> *Who but owns their magic sway,*
> *Who but knows they all decay!*
> *The tender thrill, the pitying tear,*
> *The generous purpose nobly dear,*
> *The gentle look that Rage disarms,*
> *These are all Immortal charms.*

Burns followed this tender song with a letter (Chambers's dating, December 1787; Fergusson's dating, 6 November 1787) from Edinburgh: 'I just now have read yours. The poetic compliments I pay cannot be misunderstood. They are neither of them so particular as to point *you* out to the world at large; and the circle of your acquaintances will allow all I have said. Besides I have complimented you chiefly, almost solely, on your mental charms. Shall I be plain with you? I will; so look to it. Personal attractions, madam, you have much above par; wit, understanding and worth, you possess in the first class. This is a cursed flat way of telling you these truths, but let me hear no more of your timidity.' Margaret Chalmers's 'timidity', of course, refers to the proposed publication of the songs he had written in her honour.

For all Burns devotees who study his relationship with Margaret Chalmers, there must come the inevitable question: What effect on Burns would marriage with Margaret Chalmers have had?

On the surface it is uncertain. Long after the poet died in 1796, Margaret Chalmers (then Mrs Lewis Hay—she married one of the partners of the Banking House of Sir William Forbes, J. Hunter & Co., 1788) told the poet Thomas Campbell (who told Dr Carruthers, who in turn told Burns's editor, Scott Douglas) that Burns had proposed marriage to her, and that she had rejected him: She did not give any reasons, but it is probable that she was already secretly engaged to Lewis Hay. There is some corroborative evidence for this: for on 17 January 1787, Burns wrote to Margaret's kinsman Gavin Hamilton that, 'He had met a "Lothian farmer's daughter" ', whom he had almost persuaded to accompany him to the west country. Thus the reason for Burns's second visit to Harvieston may have been to further woo the undecided Margaret.

In Agnes Maclehose's opinion Margaret Chalmers would have been an ideal wife for Burns;* at least she could have given Burns much that Jean Armour could never have done: One thinks of intellectual companionship and social elevation as two probable and readily identifiable benefits.

Lewis Hay died in 1800 leaving Margaret Chalmers with six children; twenty years later she went to Pau (in the foothills of the Pyrenees) for her health and died at the age of 80 or so in 1843.

Even today there remains something odd about the Burns affair with Margaret Chalmers. Claimed as his last poetical effort dated 'Brow, on the Solway Furth, 12 July 1796' was this (to the tune Rothiemurchie):

---

* See: Brown, Raymond Lamont. *Clarinda*, pp. 114–15 and 155.

Chorus
Fairest maid on Devon banks,
Crystal Devon, winding Devon,
Wilt thou lay that frown aside,
And smile as thou wert wont to do.

I
Full well thou knowest I love thee dear,
Couldst thou to malice lend an ear!
O did not Love exclaim, 'Forbear,
'Nor use a faithful lover so'.—

II
Then come, thou fairest of the fair,
Those wanton smiles O let me share;
And by thy beauteous self I swear,
No love but thine my heart shall know.—

And it has left us with an enigma. If the poem was newly
written at the time (which I doubt), it shows that even *in extremis*
he had a final nostalgic thought or two for Margaret Chalmers; but
more important, it shows what she must have meant to him, and
how much he must have suffered and lost by her rejection of his
'assiduities'.

Appendix III

The Humble Petition of Bruar Water

The poem was originally published unsigned in *The Edinburgh Magazine*, X (Nov. 1789), pp. 317–18. Josiah Walker may have sent it to the editor. William Scott Douglas in his 1871 edition of Burns's *Works* noted:

> This lively and characteristic production was very rapidly composed by Burns in the course of his north tour in company with Nicol in 1787. He reached Blair Castle, the seat of the Duke of Athole, and was a guest there till Monday morning, 3rd September. On 5th September, on reaching Inverness, he wrote to Mr Josiah Walker, tutor to the Duke's family (afterwards Professor Walker of Glasgow University), enclosing the poem, with the remarks: 'I have just time to write the foregoing, and to tell you that it was—at least most part of it—the effusion of a half-hour I spent at Bruar. I do not mean it was *extempore*, for I have endeavoured to brush it up as well as Mr Nicol's chat and the jogging of the chaise would allow. It eases my heart a good deal, as rhyme is the coin with which a poet pays his debts of honour or gratitude.' The two days Burns spent at Blair he afterwards declared to be among the happiest days of his life. Professor Walker has recorded that 'he tried to exert his abilities, because he knew that it was ability alone that gave him a title to be there'.

> *My Lord, I know, your noble ear*
> *Woe ne'er assails in vain;*
> *Embolden'd thus, I beg you'll hear*
> *Your humble slave complain,*
> *How saucy Phebus' scorching beams,*
> *In flaming summer-pride,*
> *Dry-withering, waste my foamy streams,*
> *And drink my crystal tide.*

The lightly-jumping, glowrin trouts,
  That thro' my waters play,
If, in their random, wanton spouts,
  They near the margin stray;
If, hapless chance! they linger lang,
  I'm scorching up so shallow,
They're left, the whitening stanes amang,
  In gasping death to wallow.

Last day I grat wi' spite and teen,
  As Poet BURNS came by,
That, to a Bard, I should be seen
  Wi' half my channel dry:
A panegyric rhyme, I ween,
  Even as I was he shor'd me;
But, had I in my glory been,
  He, kneeling, wad ador'd me.

Here, foaming down the skelvy rocks,
  In twisting strength I rin;
There, high my boiling torrent smokes,
  Wild-roaring o'er a linn:
Enjoying large each spring and well
  As Nature gave them me,
I am, altho' I say't mysel,
  Worth gaun a mile to see.

Would then my noble master please
  To grant my highest wishes,
He'll shade my banks wi' towering trees,
  And bonie spreading bushes.
Delighted doubly then, my Lord,
  You'll wander on my banks,
And listen mony a grateful bird
  Return you tuneful thanks.

The sober laverock, warbling wild,
  Shall to the skies aspire;
The gowdspink, Music's gayest child,
  Shall sweetly join the choir;
The blackbird strong, the lintwhite clear,
  The mavis mild and mellow;
The robin pensive Autumn chear,
  In all her locks of yellow.

This too, a covert shall ensure,
To shield them from the storm;
And coward maukin sleep secure,
Low in her grassy form:
Here shall the shepherd make his seat,
To weave his crown of flowers;
Or find a sheltering, safe retreat,
From prone-descending showers.

And here, by sweet endearing stealth,
Shall meet the loving pair,
Despising worlds with all their wealth
As empty idle care:
The flowers shall vie in all their charms
The hour of heaven to grace,
And birks extend their fragrant arms
To screen the dear embrace.

Here haply too, at vernal dawn,
Some musing bard may stray,
And eye the smoking, dewy lawn,
And misty mountain, gray;
Or, by the reaper's nightly beam,
Mild-chequering thro' the trees,
Rave to my darky dashing stream,
Hoarse-swelling on the breeze.

Let lofty firs, and ashes cool,
My lowly banks o'erspread,
And view, deep-bending in the pool,
Their shadows' wat'ry bed:
Let fragrant birks, in woodbines drest,
My craggy cliffs adorn;
And, for the little songster's nest,
The close embowering thorn.

So may, Old Scotia's darling hope,
Your little angel band
Spring, like their fathers, up to prop
Their honour'd native land!
So may, thro' Albion's farthest ken,
To social-flowing glasses
The grace be—'Athole's honest men,
'And Athole's bonnie lasses!'

Selected Bibliography

Anderson, P. J. *Officers and Graduates of University and King's College, Aberdeen*. Aberdeen: nd.

Bain, George. *History of Nairnshire*. Nairn: Telegraph Office, 1893.

Brown, Raymond Lamont. *Clarinda: The Intimate Story of Robert Burns and Agnes Maclehose*. Dewsbury: MB Publications, 1968.

Bulloch, Joseph G. B. *A History of Genealogy of the family of Baillie of Dunain, Dochfour and Lamington*. Green Bay, Wisconsin: 1898.

Bullock, John M. *William Marshall, the Scots Composer, 1748–1833*. Inverness: Carruthers, 1933.

Burns Chronicle, The. Volumes for 1893, 1904, 1906, 1919, 1927, 1944.

Campbell, Duncan. *The Lairds of Glenlyon*. Place and publisher unknown: 1886.

Campbell, Nancie. *The Murison Burns Collection*. Dunfermline: Dunfermline Public Libraries, 1953.

Chambers, Robert. *The Life and Works of Robert Burns*. Edinburgh: W. & R. Chambers, 1856, Vol. II.

Chambers Edinburgh Journal. 11 January 1940.

Daiches, David. *Robert Burns and his world*. London: Thames & Hudson, 1971.

Douglas, William Scott. *The Works of Robert Burns*. Edinburgh: Paterson, 1878.

Drummond, P. R. *Perthshire in Bygone Days*. London: Whittingham, 1879.

Dundee Advertiser. Letters sequence 23 February–1 March 1922.

Ewing, J. C. *Journal of a tour in the Highlands made in the year 1787*. Glasgow: Gowans & Gray, 1927.

Fergusson, J. De Lancey. *The Letters of Robert Burns*. London: Oxford University Press, 1931, Vol. I, 1780–89; Vol. II, 1790–96.

Fitzhugh, Robert T. *Robert Burns: The Man and The Poet.* London: W. H. Allen, 1971.

Glasgow Herald. Death of Dr Wallace. Glasgow, 1921.

Groome, Francis. *Ordnance Gazetteer. Scotland,* Vol. I, 1884.

Harvey, William. *Robert Burns in Stirlingshire.* Stirling: Eneas Mackay, 1899.

Hay, George. *Round about the Round 'O' with its poets.* Arbroath: Buncle, 1888.

Hempstead, James L. *Dumbarton men of wisdom who honoured Burns in his Lifetime.* Dumbarton: *County Reporter,* 1972.

Horn, Barbara L. H. *Letters of John Ramsay, 1799–1812.* Edinburgh: Scottish History Society, 1966.

Inglis, John Alexander. *The Munros of Auchinbowie and Cognate Families.* Edinburgh: T. & A. Constable, 1911.

Innes, C. *A Genealogical Deduction of the Family of Rose of Kilravock.* Edinburgh: no imprint, 1848.

Irving, Joseph. *The History of Dumbartonshire.* Dumbarton: printed privately, 1860.

Lindsay, Maurice. *Robert Burns: The man, his work, the legend.* London: Macgibbon & Kee, 1954.

Lindsay, Maurice. *The Burns Encyclopaedia.* London: Hutchinson, 1959, 1970.

MacFarlan, Robert. *Burns in Dumbarton.* Dumbarton: reprinted privately from the *Dumbarton Herald* of 14 February 1912.

Macleod, Donald. *Dumbarton Ancient and Modern.* Glasgow: Maclure, Macdonald & Co., 1893.

Marshall, William. *Historic Scenes in Perthshire.* Edinburgh: William Oliphant & Co., 1880.

Robertson, James. *A History of Burns's Forefathers, his travels in Scotland and his Masonic Affairs.* Aberdeen: published privately, 1949.

Rodger, Robert. *Dumbarton Burns Club, 1859–1959.* Dumbarton: Bennett & Thomson, 1959.

Royal Commission of Ancient and Historical Monuments of Scotland: Stirlingshire volumes.

Scott, Hew. *Fasti Ecclesiae Scotianae.* Edinburgh: Oliver & Boyd, 1925.

Stewart, Elizabeth. *Dunkeld: An Ancient City.* Dunkeld: Munro Press, 1926.

Strachey, Lady (editor). *Memoirs of a Highland Lady.* London: John Murray, 1898.

Tocher, J. F. *The Tour of the North-East in 1787.* 'Immortal Memory' to the Burns Banff Club, 1931. From the photostat copy held by Banff County Library, 1972.

Walker, William. *The Bards of Bon-Accord, 1375–1860.* Aberdeen: Edmond & Spark, 1887.

Willis, R. L. *A Tour from London to Elgin, 1790.* London: Thomson, 1897.

Index

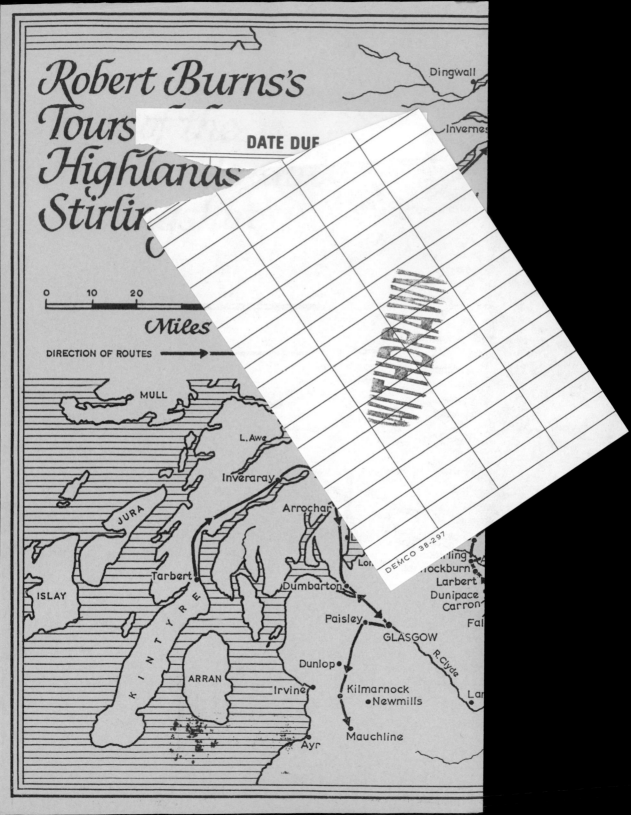